## DANTE'S PURGATORIO

Philip Terry was born in Belfast, and is a poet, translator, and a writer of fiction. He has translated the work of Georges Perec, Michèle Métail and Raymond Queneau, and is the author of the novel tapestry, shortlisted for the Goldsmiths Prize. His poetry and experimental translations include *Oulipoems*, *Dante's Inferno* and *Dictator*, a version of the *Epic of Gilgamesh* in Globish. *The Penguin Book of Oulipo*, which he edited, was published in Penguin Modern Classics in 2020, and Carcanet published his edition of Jean-Luc Champerret's *The Lascaux Notebooks*, the first ever anthology of Ice Age poetry, in 2022.

**ALSO BY PHILIP TERRY FROM CARCANET**

The Lascaux Notebooks, Jean-Luc Champerret, translator (2022)
Dictator (2018)
Quennets (2016)
Dante's Inferno (2014)
Shakespeare's Sonnets (2010)
Elementary Morality, Raymond Queneau, translator (2008)

# Dante's Purgatorio

Philip Terry

CARCANET POETRY

First published in Great Britain in 2024 by
Carcanet
Alliance House, 30 Cross Street
Manchester, M2 7AQ
www.carcanet.co.uk



A CIP catalogue record for this book is available from the British Library.

ISBN 978 1 80017 445 0

Book design by Andrew Latimer, Carcanet
Typesetting by LiteBook Prepress Services
Printed in Great Britain by SRP Ltd, Exeter, Devon

FSC www.fsc.org MIX Paper | Supporting responsible forestry FSC® C014540

The publisher acknowledges financial assistance from Arts Council England.

Supported using public funding by ARTS COUNCIL ENGLAND

## CONTENTS

## CANTO I

For better waters, now, the little smack
Of my inwit hoists its sail
Leaving behind the bottomlesss gulf,

Whose misery gouged deep its keel.
I will sing now of that strange island
Where the good dead are made better

And beaten into pure form,
Becoming fit to build on Earth a better place.
Oh Oulipo, who set free my voice,

Here let dead poetry live again,
And let Calliope sing along with that sweet
Contralto, whose strain shut the magpies up for good.

Like a photoshopped image of dawn
The radiant light of the sunshine coast
Burst from the horizon,

Blinding my dimmed sight with its refulgence,
So that I had to narrow the slits of my eyes
Which had grown accustomed to Hell's dark.

Like distant laughter,
The planet Beckett described in *Ill Seen Ill Said*
Rose above the fishing boats anchored offshore.

I turned to the right, fixing my peepers on the
Other pole,
          where I saw four wind turbines gleaming:

The sky seemed to welcome their giant forms
As their blades began to turn
Bringing clean energy across the waters.

When I had finished gawping, I checked the football
On my phone – the ball was passed back in front of goal,
To where Wayne should have been, but he was gone.

I saw nearby an old man, standing alone,
        his hair was all white,
                        his complexion bright,

And as I gazed into his eyes I recognised
Once more a man I had met on Earth,
The tenant of Bottengoms, author of *Akenfield*.

The breeze that swept across the shore
                                lofted his hair
Like a rock star's in front of a wind-machine.

'Who are you, travellers, who have escaped
The eternal prison inside the Knowledge Gateway?'
He said, eyeing us haughtily.

'How did you get here, against the blind current,
Or have the bus routes changed,
Or the laws of the VC been broken?

Is there a new edict in Senate such that
The damned, on day release, may wander into my
Caravan Park unchecked, from the Infernal Campus?'

Berrigan, my guide, seized me from behind,
And with a word in my ear and a nudge with his knee
Made me bend down and pay my respects.

Then he replied: 'I didn't come here of my
Own volition. A lady from London, lauded by
Knopfler – you may know the song, "Lady Writer" –

Asked me to help this man out of a fix.
But since you're asking what the Hell
We're doing here, let me put you straight.

This man has yet to pop his clogs,
But, through his misfortune, was so damn close to death
That there was barely time to turn things round.

As I've said, I was sent
To rescue him, and the only way was down,
The only way was Essex.

Already I have shown him all the damned souls
In the Infernal Campus, now I want him to see the good dead
Who come to rehab, here on the Essex coast.

How we got here?
How long have you got, old man? Put it this way –
When we set out on our journey through Hell,

Three days since, nobody had heard of Covid-19,
And now I've got a signal on my phone it's all I read about.
From the AHRC comes the funding that brings him here,

So don't think about turning us back,
Make us welcome, like refugees fleeing a warzone,
We've seen some shit, so give us a break man.

Senate's edicts have no hold on us;
For this man still lives, and I am no lackey of Landman.
I'm from the same zone as your friend Imogen Holst –

Along with another bunch of artists –
She still talks fondly of you, so for her sake,
If for no other reason,

Let us travel through your seven zones.
I'll give her a big hug for you
If you don't grudge being mentioned in that place.'

'Three days, you say,' he mumbled,
'I think you've been in Hell longer than you think,
But time can do funny things down there.'

Then he pulled on a face mask and approached us gingerly,
Pointing a temperature gun at our chests.
'Looks like your Covid-free, but I have to be sure,'

He said. 'Like New Zealand, this island is
Virus-free, but I mean to keep it that way.
Any arrivals from the mainland have to self-isolate

Before making the trip over the water,
And we check them once more on disembarkation,
We don't want to take any unnecessary risks.'

Relaxing a little, he went on: 'When I was working
For dear Ben at the Aldeburgh Festival in its infancy
Imo was so pleasing to my eyes

That everything she asked of me I did.
Now that she dwells beyond the evil river
She can no longer move me, such things are governed

By an immutable law buried in the university charter.
But if this lady from London, winner of the Holberg Prize,
Moves and commands you, just ask in her name.

Go then, and see that you hitch up this man's
Trousers – a smooth rush should do it – and wipe off
All this filth

That has so clouded his face
He looks like a paramilitary:
To climb this mountain you'll need to look smart.

All around the border of this little island,
There where the waves erode the shore,
Are rushes growing out of soft clay.

No other plants that put forth leaf or lignin
Are able to thrive here, for they cannot
Yield to the constant buffeting of the North Sea.

Once you're done, don't return by this way.
The sun, which just now is rising,
Will show you the best route to tackle this mountain.'

With that, he disappeared; and I stood up,
Without a word, dusted myself down,
And rejoined Berrigan who was lighting a smoke.

He took a draw, then said: 'Let's go dude, we must turn back,
The beach here slopes down to the shore,
Beyond the remains of the old Block House.'

The dawn crackled,
                                        dissolving the morning mist,
Which rose then vanished in the air.

We plodded on across the lonely beach,
As people looking for some precious object they have lost –
Like a couple I once saw in Snape who lost their wedding ring –

Until we reached a shady part where the
Dew resting on the banks of grass still lingered.
Here Berrigan grunted, and kneeling down in the wetness

He held out both his outstretched palms
And rubbed them all over the grass:
When I saw what he was about

I stepped over and offered him my cheeks
Which were stained with tears, and there,
Applying his hands like a masseur

He once more brought to light my native
Complexion which Hell had hidden.
We came then onto the deserted shore

Which never saw any sail upon its waters
That belonged to the land of the living.
Then Berrigan bent down and plucked

A stiff rush, wincing as it cut into his poet's hands,
And tied it round my middle like a belt.
And when he plucked this humble plant,

Miraculously, it renewed itself before my eyes,
Like some genetically modified crop that can
Copy itself once harvested,

There, in the very place from where he had taken it.

## CANTO II

'Now,' said Berrigan,
'The sunrise in these parts, they say,
Is awesome – let's check it out!'

As he spoke he took out his gear
And hunkered down on the beach
To skin up.

'Look at those colours, dude,' he drawled,
Handing me the smoke,
And as I took a draw

I swear the dawn changed colour
Now yellow, now pink, now deep orange,
As it filled the horizon.

We were still sitting there by the water's new day,
Like stoners, absorbed in the now,
Not even thinking what our next steps might be,

When suddenly I saw, low from the north
(Like the red glow of Bradwell that burns at dawn
Through the dense haze that hovers on the sea)

A light – so may I see it again! –
A bright light, travelling like lightning
Over the sea, far faster than any jet ski.

I turned to question Berrigan, my guide,
But he just sat there cross-legged, without moving,
Like some Buddhist monk, toying with his beard,

Then when I looked back I saw the light
Both brighter and bigger grown.
Then, on each side of it,

I began to make out some white thing,
And beneath it too, little by little,
Another whiteness became visible.

Berrigan sat there without uttering a word,
Until the moment when the first white things
Became clearly visible – they were wings! –

And beneath them hung two floats, the
Landing gear of what looked like an amphibious plane,
And when he recognised the craft, Berrigan cried:

'Now bend your knees! That plane's the *Angel di*
*Dio*, and if I'm not mistaken the pilot's Amy Johnson,
The first woman to fly solo from London to Australia.

See how close to the water she flies! How
Tightly she turns! Those goggles, that scarf,
That flying helmet, I'd recognise them anywhere!'

Then as more and more towards us came
The bird divine, brighter yet it appeared,
With the brightening beam of the rising sun behind,

And I had to look down
                    not to be blinded
                                        by the glare.

Johnson brought the craft down on the water,
So gently slicing through the waves
That there was no backwash at all.

I could now see the pilot clearly in the cockpit,
And all the faces peering out,
There must have been at least a hundred

Packed in there, as if they'd been taking a lesson
From Ryanair,
                    and as they touched down

They sang together with a single voice:
*'We are the champions, my frie-end!'*
With all that follows those words on the album sleeve.

Then she pulled a lever above her head
And the cabin doors slid open, no, they *became* slides,
The passengers sliding out into rubber dinghies,

Which inflated at a touch, propelling them to the strand.
Moments later, and she was gone,
Her cargo stranded on the shore.

Men in white bodysuits and goggles,
Holding infrared thermometers, met them,
To check their temperatures as they passed.

The throng left there seemed not to understand
What place it was, or what was happening, but stood
And stared about like refugees arriving in a new land.

The sun, which with the infra-red in each ray,
Had chased the vapour trails from the height of Heaven,
On every hand was shooting forth the day,

When one of those new souls looked up to where
Berrigan and I stood on the strand, saying to us:
'If you know it, show us the road that leads

Off the beach and takes us up the Essex Alp.'
To which Berrigan replied with a drawl:
'If you think that we're from around these parts,

Think again, stranger, we are aliens like yourself.
We arrived but now, a little before you,
By a way that was so rough and hard

The climb that lies ahead will seem like child's play.'
The creatures, who must have clocked from my breathing
That I was still alive, stood gawping in amazement, and

As to some messenger in an antique play, who bears
The olive, people draw near to hear the news,
So on my face those pilgrims fixed their gaze,

Those fortunate ones, momentarily forgetting why
They had come to this strange island.
As they stood there staring I wondered what

Had brought them to their ends – some, by the look
Of them, had died from old age, but among their numbers
Were many who had died young,

Their lives cut short by leukaemia, cancer,
Cirrhosis of the liver, a crash on the roads, Covid-19.
One of them I saw breaking the ranks,

And he stepped forward to embrace me
With such great warmth
That he moved me to do the like.

Oh shades empty save in outward show!
Three times behind its form I clasped my hands,
Three times they returned to my sides through empty air.

With wonder, I believe, I must have changed colour,
Because the shade smiled ironically, then drew back,
Unable, at last, to contain its laughter.

Then he told me not to waste my time, he was
A shade, and by his voice I knew who he was,
And begged him to stop a while to talk to me.

'Just as I had time for you when I was in my mortal body,
At least when that body wasn't getting some nookie,
So I have time for you now, friend. But what brings you

To this place? Spill the beans.' 'Aaron, my old shipmate,
I make this journey, how shall I put it, to *find* myself,
Accompanied by this ancient poet, but what brings you

Here, at this moment?' 'For some time now I've been
Shored up in one of the pubs in Brightlingsea, The Railway
Tavern – maybe you know it? – playing lead guitar with

The Vibrators, who're back on the road, yet for three weeks now,
Just as Merkel took in refugees in 2016, they've been letting
Anyone cross the water who was up for the trip,

And so it was that I took my turn to wait
On the foreshore, self-isolating, there where the waters
Of the Colne grow salt, and arrived just now with our pilot.

For that same shore now she has set her sat nav,
Because crowds gather there all day long,
All who do not sink down to the Infernal Campus.'

And I: 'If some new law governing this place,
Or your disembodied form, does not prevent you
Playing that guitar you carry, as you used to,

Please, take that instrument out of its case,
And give us a tune, if only for old time's sake!'
Then he took out his guitar, as we sat on the strand,

And started to sing 'Flagmen',
With a voice that was a little rusty,
But on guitar he was still note perfect:

*'Wet grass, and a co-old night,*
*Flat shadows run in front of blue lights,*
*Flags broke and splintered,*

*Saw voices in the dark –*
*They became a fighting uuunit…'*
We were all fixed on his performance,

Getting into the groove,
When, what do you know, Ronald Blythe showed up,
To put a stop to the party. 'What's going on?' he said,

'This is no time for a beach party. You won't catch
Coronavirus on this island – like Guernsey, like New Zealand,
We're Covid-free, but that's no reason

To forget where you are and why you've come here.
There's work to do! Come, you need to get yourselves
Off the beach, and ready yourselves for the climb.'

As ravers breaking lockdown, pumping the air with crazed fists
In some Devon barn, turn pale and flee
When the police raid the joint, running to their vehicles,

So, at that moment, did those newly arrived souls
Turn white
            and pick themselves up off the sand

Moving
      one by one
                  towards the sea wall bounding the island.

Nor was our parting less quick.

## CANTO III

Those frightened souls now scattered across the shore,
Legging it over the sand towards the Essex Peak
Where the good dead learn to climb,

While I, as we ran, not knowing what to do,
Stuck close to Berrigan, my guide,
For who else could show me the way?

He looked, when at last we stopped, completely out of puff,
Standing, bent, with his hands on his knees,
Red-faced, wheezing.

Then, when he stood up, lighting a smoke,
Now free of that haste which mars our dignity,
My mind, which had been caught up in the adrenaline rush,

Now relaxed, and I looked around at ease. Towering above
The shore, like nothing I had seen before, like nothing,
Certainly, I had seen in *Essex*, rose a great craggy peak,

While blazing red with its light behind us, the sun
Outlined my human shape on the sand
In front of me, as my body obstructed its rays,

And seeing only before *me* the earth darkened,
I turned around in panic,
Fearing I had been abandoned.

'Loosen up,' said Berrigan, my guide,
'I'm not about to walk out on you now,
Not after all we've been through.

It is still night time over Calverton National Cemetery
Where my body, that once cast a shadow, is buried;
From Greenwich Village to Long Island it was moved.

If now I cast no shadow before me,
Don't look so amazed. It's no stranger than
The fact the sun's rays don't block each other out.

Yet bodies such as mine are still sensitive
To pain and cold and heat –
And we still get out of breath, as you see.

Get used to it – there's another world,
A world of spirits, running parallel
To the real world.

It's the same in the infernal region we left,
For in the material world the real
University still carries on its business

As Vice-Chancellors come and go.
Materialists don't accept this,
That's why they live without hope, in desire –

You met some of them down below,
Richard Bartle, Roy Trubshaw, and
The astronaut Rodolfo Vela,

And there are many others,
Not just those with Essex connections
That I showed you.

But you met them at the start of our
Journey, I may have glossed over
Some of this, just to keep things simple.'

Ted bent his head for a moment, staring at the earth,
He looked pissed off, but I don't know what was eating him –
Maybe that I was a slow learner? Maybe something else?

By now we had come to the shore's limit
And there we found a sandy cliff so steep and slippery
The nimblest legs would not have served you there.

The craggiest, the cruellest precipice,
On the slopes of Ben Nevis would seem,
Compared to this, inviting stairs to climb.

'How are we to know,' said Berrigan my guide,
'Just where this cliff face might let us climb,
So that those without crampons might ascend?'

While he stood there, head bent,
Wondering how we should best proceed,
And I was gazing up at this wall of sand –

Along the base of the cliff, to my left,
A crowd of shades was inching towards us,
Who seemed barely to advance, they came so slowly,

Like victims of Long Covid. 'Master,' I said, 'take a
Look over there! These climbers advancing over the
Strand might show us the way if you think we're lost!'

He looked up, his face now free from doubt,
And said: 'Let's go and meet them', they move so slowly,
Buck up now, they might just have a map.'

After we'd trudged the sand for a good five minutes,
The crowd were still as far off
As Peter Shilton might kick a ball upfield,

When, all of a sudden, they pressed close to the
Sandy cliff, standing still, huddled together,
As one halts who sees some peril ahead.

They looked like climbers, for the most part, kitted out
With all the gear – ropes, helmets, and bright blue boulder mats –
Though some wore dark cloaks, like priests or wizards.

'Hey there, you! You the good dead, who are
Already chosen,' Berrigan called, 'by that same peace
Which I believe you are all in search of,

Tell us where this cliff slopes, so that
We can get a foothold on it – we are climbers
Like you, and wish to go up the mountain.'

As sheep come forth from the fold, in ones,
In twos, in threes, and the others hold back,
Casting their eyes and noses about,

And what the first one does, the others copy,
Huddling up to her if she stands still,
Silly and quiet and knowing not why,

So then we witnessed the leader of that flock
Take a step in our direction,
Modest in look, head held high.

Yet when those in the fore saw the light
Broken on the ground to my right side
So that the shadow fell from me dancing over the cliff,

They halted and drew back, and
All the others that came behind did likewise,
Not knowing why.

'Before you ask let me tell you that this
Is a human body that you see
By which the sun's light on the sand is cleft.

Don't stand there gawping – it is not
Without help from a high place
That this soul looks to climb this wall.'

So said Berrigan, my guide, and the climbers replied:
'Come, this way, where there's a path up the cliff,'
Gesturing to us with their hands.

Then one of them began with a cavernous voice: 'Whoe're thou
Art who journey'st this way, thy visage turn;
Think if my face thou hast seen in the history books?'

Startled, I turned towards him, looking him up and down.
He wore a grey cloak and a blue cap, like some
Medieval pilgrim, and he had a gentle face,

Except there was a gash under one of his eyes.
I had to confess, embarrassed, I didn't have a clue who
He was, at which point he turned to me:

'Now behold!' he said, pulling back his cloak
To reveal great cuts where his arms began,
'I am John Ball, of Colchester, Bishop of the People,

Who helped the peasants rise up against their oppressors.
The stories told about me are many, but when you have returned
To the Earth, tell them what you heard from me,

If other tales are still told. When by five mortal blows
My frame fell, my body was dismembered,
The parts dispersed to four corners of England –

Coventry, Chester, York and Canterbury –
So that none may make vigil at my grave.
When these blows my frame had shattered,

I betook myself weeping to Him who of free will
Forgives. My sins were many, if less than my enemies claim,
But so wide arms hath goodness infinite,

That they receive all who turn to them.
Had this text divine been of Sudbury better scann'd,
Who excommunicated me for free preaching,

My body would yet lie in one place, 'neath hallow'd ground.
Yet by such curses are we not so destroyed,
But that the eternal love may turn, while hope

Retains her verdant blossom. True it is, withal,
That such a one as in contumacy dies
Against holy Church, though he repent,

Must wander thirtyfold for all the time
In his presumption past; if such decree be
Not by prayers of good men shorter made.

Things cannot go aright in England and ne'er will
Until goods are held in common and there are no
More villeins and gentlefolk but we all are the same.

Look therefore if thou canst advance my bliss,
Revealing to your age how thou beheldst me,
And the terms laid on me of that interdict,

For here from those below much profit comes.'

## CANTO IV

When you're completely engrossed in a movie
On Netflix, or sitting on the edge of your seat
Watching a football game,

Or if you're involved in a road accident, say,
Your car spinning out of control into a ditch,
Or straight into a tree, you lose all sense of time,

So caught up in the moment are you
That time itself seems to expand
As a gas expands to fill all the available space –

Something which never happens
                    when you're multitasking
And which is alien to the business mindset.

I was now experiencing this for myself
As I listened, marvelling, to the words of John Ball –
For the sun had risen a good 45° into the sky

And I had not even clocked it –
When, at a certain point along the way, these climbers
Cried out in a single voice: 'Here's what you're looking for!'

A bigger opening is often closed up by a
Bricklayer, while his apprentice stops for a fag
Break, than that narrow gap we now climbed through,

Berrigan, my guide, first, I after him,
Followed close by the climbers
                    with a weary tread.

Maum Turk Mountains you can scale, edge up
Mount Gable, climb to Dunluce Castle, ascend Errigal.
Feet will do there, but here you must scramble on hands

And knees. Squeezed between crumbling walls of sand,
We struggled upwards through that eroding cliff wall,
Clinging to roots when our foothold gave way.

Behind us the climbers took out their picks,
Using these to haul themselves upwards,
Securing footholds with crampons, throwing back ropes.

Once we emerged on the upper edge of this
Sandy cliff, once more on open ground,
'Berrigan,' I said, 'where do we go now?'

And he replied: 'Do not lose your nerve now, we
Must keep straight on if we wish to climb the mountain,
But first we must stop at the Visitors' Centre,

Where we can get a hold of a pass and some maps,
Until we find a more experienced guide.'
The mountain, from here, rose up higher than I could see,

Disappearing into the cloud layer, and as I looked I stumbled
Back, overcome by vertigo. When I had pulled myself together,
I said to Berrigan, voicing what was bugging me:

'Tell me, I'm confused, I thought we were on Mersea Island,
But this mountain is like something you'd find in the Alps,
Or the Pyrenees, or in Northern Spain – Essex is flat!'

'Listen,' said Berrigan, 'you're forgetting what I said before,
About the spirit world running parallel to the real world: this
Is not the *real* Mersea, where Jos Williams moors his boat,

And where he teaches courses on astronavigation
To the young sailors of West Mersea, so that they can,
Without the aid of GPS, travel safely across the ocean,

But a parallel Mersea, in a parallel Essex. In this Essex
There are mountains, some of the highest in the world,
But who knows, in some divergent future there may well be

Mountains in the real Essex, whether thrown up by the
Wivenhoe fault, or by the intervention of climate artists,
For much of this landscape is under threat from the sea,

And mountains not only form a barrier against erosion,
But aid habitat development, and precipitation, as well as
Carbon balancing, coz of the flora and fauna they support.

But don't be so amazed – this journey will require
A willing suspension of disbelief, as Coleridge says,
Which he defines as *poetic faith*. When you get

Back, you should check out his *Biographia Literaria*
If you don't know it – it's got some real pearls.
Now, let's make tracks for the Visitors' Centre.'

Already, ahead of us, we could see some of the climbers
Making their way across the grass, some peeling
Off towards the Caravan Park, others purchasing tickets

For Magic Puffin, or to make their way up the mountain.
When we'd caught up, we went into the shop to ask for help.
They gave us a Guidebook and a plan, marking

A series of tracks, from Easy to Difficult,
And themed walks: The Route of the Gluttons,
Marked in red, The Way of the Indolent, marked

Blue, The Path of Excessive Love of Earthly Goods,
Marked green, and a number of others I forget.
Berrigan chose the route marked Difficult,

And we were furnished with new boots, a stick each,
And some rope which Berrigan hitched to his waist.
They gave us a little card, as well, with a Puffin logo

On the front, to be stamped as we proceeded,
Making our way up past the way-posts.
I saw Berrigan pulling something out of his breast pocket,

Which he swallowed, then in an instant he was off,
Striding energised towards the mountain.
I felt the strength draining from my legs

As I hurried to keep up. 'Berrigan,' I cried,
'Unless you slow your pace you're going to lose me –
The biggest peaks I've climbed are those outside Sheffield,

Which are nothing to this one.' 'Son,' he said,
'We need to make a brisk start. Keep climbing, past the blue
Markers, just to there' – and he pointed to a narrow ledge,

Not far above, that skirted the mountain.
His words were like a goad, and I strained on,
Behind him, on hands and knees and elbows,

Until I felt the ledge under my feet at last.
Once here, we both sat down for a smoke,
Looking back at all we had climbed.

The shore was now far below us, out at
Sea we could see tankers on the horizon, and below
New streams of climbers arriving at the Visitors' Centre.

'That was worth it,' I said, between puffs,
'For the view alone – it's something else.
But tell me, for I can't keep this pace up for long,

How much more climbing are you planning on doing?
This peak soars higher than my eyes can see.'
'This mountain,' he said, stubbing out his cigarette,

'Is not like other mountains. To begin with,
Sure, it's hard to climb, but here,
Look what it says in the Guidebook: "Climbing

The Essex Alp offers the visitor a unique
Experience: here, the more you climb,
The easier it gets – that's a guarantee –

Until the slope feels gentle to the point
That climbing becomes as effortless
As drifting down the Colne in a canoe.

At this point you will have reached
Your journey's end, and you can enjoy
A welcome rest in our visitor facilities."'

Hardly had Berrigan finished reading
When we heard a voice from nearby call: 'You'll
Need a fucking rest long before you reach any facilities!'

We turned, shocked, to where the voice had come from,
And to our left we saw a massive rock surrounded
By blue boulder mats, that we hadn't noticed before.

We went over to the rock, and behind it
There was a group of climbers sprawling in its shade,
Drinking and passing round a joint.

There was one there who looked shagged out,
Red-faced, who sat with his arms hugging
His knees, and who looked like he could go no further.

'Berrigan,' I cried, 'take a look at him!
He looks like a right skiver, what's he doing on the mountain?'
The figure then turned in our direction

With a grin, saying: 'If you're so full of beans,
Why don't you just run up to the top?'
And as I looked again, I thought I recognised

His face. Exhausted, and out of puff,
I made my way towards him with my stick, and when I
Reached his side he raised his face and said:

'What the fuck are you doing here? Since when have
You taken up mountaineering?' His laid-back
Demeanour and his sarcastic wit made me smile,

And I replied to him: 'Tony Tackling!
It's good to clap eyes on you again!
You must've picked up the mountain bug in Hong Kong!

But tell me, what are you doing just sitting
Here like this? Are you waiting for a guide?
Or just being your old self again?'

'You make me laugh,' he said,
'If I tried to go up they wouldn't let me
Through the gate – the mountain's swarming with security.

Before I make a move, the sun must revolve
As many times as when I was on Earth,
For I was always putting things off till the end.

Some people here reckon prayers can shorten
Our time here – but as I'm no believer
I think this is all bollocks.

But maybe if you write a poem for me,
Or smoke a spliff for me, or
Just think nice thoughts about me,

Or just remember me, or like my Facebook page,
For God's sake, it'll have the same effect.'
The poet had now begun to climb again,

Behind me. 'Let's shift!' he called,
'The sun has reached the meridian,
Heaven's highest point, while in

The East night sets her foot on Hong Kong's shore.'
Berrigan dug into his breast pocket, pulling out
Some pills, red ones and blue ones.

Handing me a blue one, he said:
'Swallow this, it'll help you on the climb.'
'Thanks,' I said, 'What are the red ones?'

'The red ones?' said Berrigan, 'They will kill you.'

## CANTO V

I had already put some distance between myself and
Those shades, and was following in Berrigan's heavy tread,
When at my back, pointing an outstretched finger,

One cried: 'Cop that! That slowcoach at the back!
The sunlight stops where he goes, on his left side,
See that? And he struts along like a living thing.'

On hearing these sarky words, I looked back,
And saw them marvelling at me, at me and at
My body, and at the broken sunlight.

'You know Dylan's "Tangled up in Blue"?' asked Berrigan.
'That's exactly what's happened to these souls,
They're stuck on the blue path, The Way of the Indolent.

Why let yourself get het up by their blathering?
Stick close to me, and let them talk.
Stand up straight, buddy, and keep moving,

For when a man lets his attention wander aimlessly
Towards every distraction, he loses his direction,
His will is sapped with constant change –

These shadow folk are just strings of vinegar dust.'
'OK,' I said, 'I'm on my way.' What else could I say?
I blushed, chastened by his good sense, watching my footing.

Meanwhile, across the grey slope of the mountain,
Another group of climbers approached from the horizon,
Chanting a song by the Sisters of Mercy, 'Temple of Love'.

But the moment they saw that my legs
Cut the light out in its tracks, they all stopped,
And in unison let out a long drawn-out '*OMGeeeee!*'

Then two of them broke away, like an *avant-garde*,
Running towards us and blurting out their question:
'Will you tell us what…err…*state* you are in?'

To which Berrigan, my guide, quipped: 'He's off his head,
Obviously, or what would he be doing climbing
This mountain before his days on Earth are up?

That's right – he's one of the living. If you
Were gobsmacked just now because you caught sight
Of his shadow, as I'm guessing, now you know.

And tell your mates it won't do them any harm
To show him a little respect.'
I never saw a meteor shower on a summer's night

Cut through the clear sky, or a
Hawk T1 power through the ether at Clacton Airshow,
As quickly as they sped back to their gang.

Then all together
they wheeled round,
And rushed towards us like some crazed army.

'Now look closely at all these dead souls pressing
Towards us,' said Berrigan, 'each one will have their plea.
By all means, lend them an ear, but press on regardless.'

'You,' they cried, 'who climb to the peaks
Clothed in the flesh you were born in, stop,
Hold your horses, just for a second,

Look at us, and tell us if there are any among us
That you recognise, so that you can bring back news
Of them to Earth. Hold on! Just a minute! What's the hurry?

We are all shades who met a violent death,
We were bad mothers till the end,
But just at the last turned to the good,

So that, repenting and forgiving,
We left the life below at one with our God,
Who fills us with desire to behold Him.'

I replied: 'I see your faces clearly,
Though I don't recognise anyone; but tell me,
Spirits in search of bliss, is there anything I can do to help?

Just say, and I will do it, by that peace
That I go searching for, journeying from world
To world with so great a guide as this.'

One soul replied: 'There's no need to swear to it.
We all trust in your goodness, and that
You will do what lies in your power, so help me God.

Now, speaking for myself, let me beg first:
If ever you should travel to the land
Between Tipperary and Clare,

I beg you, be so good as to ask the good souls
Of Limerick to say a prayer for George Clancy,
And give me strength to cleanse my grievous sins.

Though wrong was partaken on both sides,
I fought for the Nationalist cause, with pride, first with
The Gaelic League, then with the Irish Volunteers.

I was born in Grange, County Limerick, but
It was at Thomondgate I met my fate. I was reading
A book in bed, one of Joyce's, when the Black and Tans

Came to the house, waking us in the wee hours
With a loud banging. Against my wife's advice
I opened the door myself, and three armed men

Ordered me out the house. When I refused to listen,
One of them pushed forward and fired six times.
My wife tried to shield me, but the bullets found their mark.

I stood for a moment in the doorway, and there I fell,
In Máire's arms, watching a pool of dark
Blood fill from my own veins.'

'I pray you find what you're looking for,' another butted
In, 'on the slopes of this mountain. As for me,
You could put in a word with the Big Man as George would say.

I am Kit Marlowe, born to a shoemaker,
There are none to pray for me, not for blasphemers,
So I walk here, amidst these shades, head bowed.'

And I: 'Christ almighty! Is it really Christopher Marlowe?
Is it true, as Rowse says in the biography I read when
An undergraduate at Leeds, that you were stabbed in Deptford?

And that you were buried in an unmarked grave?'
'Ah,' he said, 'the drunken brawl! All I can say
Is that I was up to my neck in trouble,

I knew too much, and knew too many,
And somebody wanted me out o' the way.
It was that base counterfeiter Frizer who wielded the knife,

Stabbing me above the eye. I stumbl'd towards the door,
Leaving a line of blood behind me on the sawdust,
And now I lost my sight. I wrestled with my tongue,

Turning it so that, with my last breath, I uttered Mary's name.
I fell – my flesh alone remaining on the threshold.
But tell this to the living, and have it appended to

My biographies – I'll speak the truth – Faustus is not damn'd!
God's Angel laid his hands on me, while Hell's fiend cried by
My ear: "*Heavenspawn, why do you steal what is mine?*

*You prise him thence for one measly tear!*
*But while you may 'scape with his immortal part,*
*Well, I've got other plans for his remains!*"

You know how humid evaporations
Gather in the air, then, rising to meet the
Cold current, condense and fall as rain? Let me tell you.

Now came Beelzebub and many more,
Combining their malice and their charms to stir
Up mist, and dark miry vapours, and cold swirling winds,

Until the whole place, within the space of an hour,
From Deptford to Greenwich Park, was fogbound.
With dark clouds his minions charged the sky,

And saturated air turned to rain:
Water pelted down, and what the sodden earth
Repuls'd filled and overflowed the stinking gutters

And fleets, the Ravensbourne and Deptford Creek,
Whose spilling waters combin'd in confluence
Forming great torrents in the streets,

That tossed me where I lay in the gutter, undoing
That cross that my arms had made in death, as the waters
Raged to the royal and mistempered Thames.

There I lay for days, an abandoned corpse,
Before they turfed me into a cart,
And dumped me in the grave you mention, unnamed.'

Now a third soul spoke up, after the second,
Quietly: 'Remember me! My name is
Siobhan Kearney, from Goatstown, South Dublin.

You can follow my story on my Twitter stream.
Ireland made me, the cord of a Dyson
Unmade me. The man who married me,

Brian Kearney, knows all about that.'

## CANTO VI

When a game of poker breaks up, the loser,
In the cold light of day, sits there despondently,
Replaying the game in his head.

Meanwhile, the crowd leave with the winner:
One skips ahead, others pester him from behind,
Another running at his side begs to be remembered.

He presses on, their voices crowding him in;
Those he gives a handout to stop bugging him,
And this is his only escape from their pleas.

I was that unfortunate, caught in a begging-fest,
Nodding now to this one, now to that,
Buying my escape with half-hearted promises.

I saw Daniel Pearl from the *Wall Street Journal*,
Kidnapped then beheaded by Al-Qaeda; I saw
A grey-bearded Che Guevara, assassinated by the CIA.

I saw with hands stretched out, imploring,
Lady Diana, Princess of Wales, and Anthony Walker
By her side, murdered in a racist attack in Merseyside,

Whose mother, drawing on her faith, found
Forgiveness for his killers; I saw JFK, who touched
My shoulder, and close behind him Sharon Tate,

Murdered by the Manson family, pregnant
With the child of Roman Polanski,
Out of sheer hate – not for any wrong she did.

Once I was free from all those shades
Who beg that others pray for them
Or put in a word on their behalf

Back on Earth to speed them on their way,
I turned to Berrigan, my guide, and said:
'If I remember right, Ted, it seems

To me that in that interview you did
With Anne Waldman and Tim Cohn,
"To Propitiate the Gods" I think it's called,

You explicitly reject Christianity,
Yet these souls look to the power of prayer to help them.
Does this mean, then, that their hopes are in vain,

Or have I misunderstood what you said?'
'You need to chill out a bit,' said Berrigan,
'And stop fretting, as I said before.

What I was trying to say in that interview
Boils down to this – *anything goes.*
Christianity may be a load of old bunkum,

But if you really believe in it and are doing it,
Like some of these guys, then you are right,
Because it works for you and will work for you.

There's a big misconception, that your spiritual
Nature and your religious nature are different,
But they're not. And we all have spiritual natures.

It doesn't matter if you're a Christian
Or a Sheik or a lesser bodhisattva,
Or even an atheist. If an atheist

Back on Earth thinks good thoughts about
One of these dudes then that will do it.
Prayer works if you believe it, it's as simple

As that. But it has many names. From another
Angle it's all about karma – if your karma's good
It'll help you climb, and if someone just thinks

Good thoughts about you while smoking a cigarette
Or whatever, it's the same. That's why Leclerc says
"The cigarette is the prayer of our time".

It's like in *Star Wars* – if the force is with you
Things are more likely to work out.
I can't put it plainer than that.

If you still don't get it, then hang on
Until the one who can bring a spark of luminosity
To connect your intellect to the wider issue shows up.

If you don't follow me, I'm talking
About Marina. You'll see her when we get to
The top, smiling in all her radiance.'

'Berrigan,' I said, 'got you I have. Now
Let's get moving, I don't feel so tired any more.
And look, the mountain's moving into the shade.'

'As long as daytime lasts,' said Berrigan,
'We'll press on. But we won't get to the top
As quickly as you think.

Before we get there, you'll see the sun
Wheel round again from where the slopes hide it,
Preventing you from casting a shadow.

But dig that bearded shade camped out over there,
Alone, giving us the evils.
He can show us the quickest road to take.'

We made our way towards him. Oh light of New Jersey,
How self-assured and disdainful you looked,
Your steady gaze so grave and dignified!

He didn't open his mouth, but just stood there
As we shuffled towards him, looking on
Like a lion *couchant*.

Berrigan made no bones about it,
But went straight up to him asking directions.
The shade ignored my guide's questions.

Asking about our origins, where we'd been living,
Our gods, our lives, *he* questioned *us*.
Berrigan, my guide, began: 'East Village…'

And the other, till then so self-absorbed,
Suddenly burst into life: 'East Village, man,
Then we're neighbours! I'm Allen Ginsberg.'

Then laughing, and embracing each other like
Old friends who had a shared history,
The two shades started swapping news.

Ah, slavish Ireland, the home of untold grief,
Ship without a helmsman caught in a furious storm,
No sainted island, but home to backstreet abortions,

And unscrupulous nuns who abuse those in their care.
How quick the King of the Beats was to respond
To the mere sound of his sweet home's name,

By welcoming his neighbour, while now, nobody
In your bounds knows rest from sectarian hatred,
And those living under the same roof, even they

Are at each other's throats. Oh wretched Ireland,
Search all your coastal havens, probe to your windswept
And barren heart, can you find any part that is at peace?

Dig up your peat bogs and even there you'll
Find the bodies of the murdered and the slain,
Your very own Tollund men.

What matter if Bill Clinton repaired
The bridle – if the saddle's empty now!
The shame would have been less if he'd kept out of it.

You clergymen who should pursue your holy orders,
Recalling what God prescribes for you,
Stop stirring up sectarian hatred –

See how this bog pony has grown viciously wild,
Without a jockey's whip to set her straight,
Since you were stupid enough to get involved in politics.

Oh, Theresa May, why did you not take greater
Care of this unruly brute, instead of stirring up strife
By forming a coalition with the UDP?

And can you not see that leaving the EU,
Which binds together North and South, then messing
With the borders, is stirring up old divides?

May a damning judgement fall from the stars
Upon your party: one unmistakable
And strange enough to disable your successors!

You and your kind, possessed by greed for what
Power is within your grasp, have let this happen:
This discarded colony of yours has gone to waste.

Come and take a look at Dublin, where the
Kinahans and the Hutches fight it out in the streets,
Or take a trip to Limerick to meet

The Keane-Collopy gang and the
McCarthy-Dundon gang and hear all about their
Turf war fuelled by absolute and mutual hatred.

Come, you shameless scumbag, come and see these forgotten
Souls who suffer as never since the potato famine, come
And see how safe it is to walk these streets.

Come and see how people love each other here!
If you can't pity us, then come and see
The misery your blind indifference has stirred up.

Oh holy Mary mother of God, to whom
This nation turns for succour, am I allowed to ask
If your passionate eyes no longer see us?

Or is this part of a greater plan cooked up
By the divine intellect to some good end
That we are powerless to comprehend?

For the cities of Ireland are filled with bullies
And sectarians and any dolt who plays
The role of bigot can pass for a Mayor.

Belfast, my sweet Belfast! How happy you must
Be with this ranting digression, for you alone are
Well out of it – thank your industrious citizens for that!

Some people have justice in their very marrow,
They *think* before they shoot –
Your people shoot off words before bullets.

Some men balk at the thought of civic duty,
Your citizens step up to the plate before they're asked,
Shouting 'I'll gladly stand for re-election!'

Rejoice, I say to you, the craic is good,
Wealthy as you are, and wise, knowing such peace!
History bears out the truth of what I say.

Athens and Lacedaemon, where ancient laws
And civil discipline were first forged,
Showed only the faintest sign of good government

When compared to you, who make such subtle provisions
In your laws, that by the time November's half done
The agreements brokered in October are in tatters.

How often within living memory have you
Changed border arrangements, stop and search
Protocol, and shoot to kill policy?

Think carefully, and if you see the truth, you'll see
An old and sadistic headmaster suffering from
Lung cancer who finds no rest on his Bupa bed,

But tosses and turns to escape his pain.

## CANTO VII

After their greetings had been repeated
Three or four times, Ginsberg took a step back and said:
'Hold on a minute, haven't we met before?

Who are you?' And Berrigan, laughing, replied:
'Before many of these souls worthy to become
Better came to this weird mother of a mountain,

My bones were buried on Long Island.
I'm Ted Berrigan, veteran of Korea,
And veteran of Essex. We crossed paths

Many a time, we even hung out together –
I remember one beautiful day at Cherry Valley in
Particular, I think Bob Dylan was there,

And hey, I edited your friend Orlovsky's
*Clean Asshole Poems* and *Smiling Vegetable Songs*,
But I guess we were just too wrapped up in our own

Poetic worlds, too stoned too, to become close friends.'
This was the answer that my guide gave him, and
As one who suddenly beholds some strange thing

At which he marvels will at first believe,
Then doubt what his eyes tell him and mutter
'It's… – but can it really be?' so seemed Ginsberg.

Then he scratched his chin, and raised his arms
To the heavens, and now getting down on his knees,
Clasped my guide round the waist in homage.

'Oh glory of the New York School,' he said,
'You who showed with what power our language can speak,
Oh undying light of the St Marks Poetry Project,

What lucky star brings you here to my side?
If you still have the strength to speak,
Tell me if you come from Hell, and from what cloister?'

'Through all the zones of the Infernal Campus
Have I journeyed here,' he said. 'A heavenly dame
Showed me the path, and following her light I come.

Not what I taught, but where I taught,
Cost me the sight of that school you seek,
Whose entry qualifications were revealed to me too late.

There is a place in Hell made sorrowful
By darkness alone and grief without torment:
No cries of pain are heard there, just hopeless sighs.

I dwell there with retired professors
Shorn of their faculties, and materialists,
Who live on in futureless limbo;

I dwell there with Essex alumni, the great and
The good, hanging out with the poets,
Dorn, Lowell, Lopez, Oliver, Raworth.

But if you know the ropes in these parts and
Are permitted to share your knowledge, tell us
The best way to where the rehab starts for real.'

'No one dictates to us here, buddy, we're free spirits,
Free to roam as we please – so far as my legs will carry
Me, I'm at your disposal to act as your guide.

But look, the day is reaching its end, and at
Night it is forbidden to ascend, so we should
Think about finding somewhere to hunker down.

If you'll allow me, off to the right here
Is a group of souls, I could take you over to see them,
I think you'll dig meeting them.'

'What are you saying, exactly?' said Berrigan, my guide,
'If a soul wanted to climb at night, like with a torch,
Are there some bouncers who'd stop them?'

Ginsberg scraped a line on the ground with his sneaker,
Answering: 'Look! After the sun has set
You'd be hard pressed to step over this mark.

There's nothing that actually stops us climbing, no one
Confiscates our ropes, but you do get zombies in these
Parts, escaped from the Infernal Campus.

You can, by all means, go *down* the mountain,
Even all the way to the beach if you wish,
While the horizon blocks out the daylight.

But even here you'll need to look out for the
Undead attracted to Essex by the spurious
Marketing: "Alight here for Bright Ideas!"

“Alight here for Spiritual Incineration!” more like,
But don’t get me started, you know what I mean.’
Berrigan, my guide, amazed at what he heard,

Replied: ‘In that case, take us to the place
You mentioned just now where we should at least
Be able to get stoned for old time’s sake.’

We started on our way, and soon I saw
A hollow vale open up beyond a crest
In the mountain, like a VIP campsite.

A winding path, that was not very steep,
Led to a vantage point on the hollow’s rim,
From where we had a clear view of the site.

There were canvas tepees, and silver
And gold boutique caravans, brightly
Painted shepherd’s huts in cochineal

And burnt amber and dusted moss,
And the brilliant colours of the grass and
The flowers and the trees in that vale

Outshone all of those, as nature surpasses art.
But it was not only a pretty picture we beheld:
The sweetness of a thousand odours

From foodstalls and camp fires filled
The night air, giving us all the munchies.
We heard voices, singing along to Leonard Cohen’s

‘Hallelujah’, and saw uncountable flags,
Bearing a Puffin logo, blowing in the gentle breeze.
‘Please don’t ask me,’ said our New Jersey guide,

'To lead you down to where you see these souls
Resting, until the sun has gone down. From here
It is much easier to get a good look at them all.

The one who is sitting on his own in front of that
Tepee, who looks like he's left something undone that
He had to do, and doesn't join the others in song,

Was Charles Stewart Parnell, who could have cured
The wounds that were the death of Ireland –
It will be some time before that land comes back to life.

The other one who seems to draw comfort from his pipe
Once occupied 10 Downing Street,
Sending the troops into Northern Ireland:

Harold Wilson – though a smoker, he's more respected
Than Heath, his old rival, is now, who the police
Would have liked to have been able to question.

That guilty-looking military figure in conference
With the kind-looking guerilla at his side,
Was the one who firebombed Dresden.

His friend, Fidel Castro, once had me deported
From Cuba for criticising a speech
In which he denounced homosexuals.

Look at Bomber Harris now, see how he beats his breast,
Sighing as he watches his transatlantic disciple
General Le May, who urged the US

To bomb North Vietnam back to the Stone Age.
That tight-lipped woman seated beside
The one with the small hands is Hilary Clinton,

Singing along with her compatriot Donald Trump.
If their kind hadn't meddled with power where
They had no right, that young man behind them there,

Salvadore Allende, would have lived to rule longer.
Jacobo Árbenz, President of Guatemala,
Was another one the CIA removed from office,

During the Eisenhower years – he got his
Kicks creating Banana Republics,
And set the tone for years of oppression

In the name of democracy and free trade. Holy shit!
It's not often that the good rise to the top,
Too many politicians are self-serving egotists.

My words apply to him with the small hands
As well as Hilary there, who sings with him,
On whose account Iraq and Afghanistan bleed.

You can argue over the details till the cows
Come home, but both of these leaders are birdbrains,
Which is what made the 2016 US Election such a farce.

Over there you'll see the Labour leader Michael Foot,
All by himself, a man who always opposed the bomb –
His line of politics bore better fruit by far.

The one who sits behind them at the bar, smoking
A cigarette and enjoying a beer, is Nigel Farage,
Whose war with the European Union

Has brought a whole nation to its knees.

## CANTO VIII

It was the hour when the fisherman's thoughts,
From out at sea, turn back towards home, and his heart
Longs for the wife he has left behind,

The hour when the commercial traveller,
Settling into his room in a new motel,
Calls his loved ones to check they are alright –

I was no longer paying attention to Ginsberg's words
But looking at a shade who had stood up
And who held a loudhailer to make herself heard.

She raised her hands into the air, and began
To clap rhythmically, stamping her foot
To the same beat, then began to sing.

'*Light up, light up!*' came from her lips,
With such a perfect and poignant melody
That it blew me off my feet; then the rest

Of the crowd, as one, joined in to sing the song
Through to the end, keeping their eyes fixed
On the sun as it sank below the horizon, each

Of them holding up lighters, which they waved in the air.
Pay attention reader, the translation now
Takes its own path, but is not hard to follow.

I saw those lucky campers, who now
In silence kept their peepers raised to the sky,
As if expectant, their faces paleflickering in the firelight,

And then I saw appear on the ridge
Two Alp Angels with powerful torches.
Over their garments they wore green capes

Which fanned out behind them in the breeze.
One took her stand above us, on our side,
And one took up a position on the opposite bank.

My eyes could make out clearly their silhouettes,
But could not bear the brightness of their torches:
Light that makes visible can also blind.

'Our friends come from the Visitors' Centre,'
Said Ginsberg, 'to guard the campsite against
Souls who try to break in without paying.

This is the hour when they show their faces.'
Clueless as to where they might appear, I looked about,
Standing close to that shade I could trust.

Ginsberg winked, then pinched my bottom, which I
Thought strange, but I didn't dare say anything.
Then he produced a fat spliff, broken short and blunted

At the end, lit it, and passed it to me. 'It's time to
Join those noble shades below,' he said, 'this will heighten
The experience. Come, they'll be dying to talk to you.'

I only had to take five or six steps,
I think, before I reached the bottom. There was
A shade there who was staring right into my face,

As if he thought he half-recognised me.
By now the air was both cold and dark, but
Not so dark that I couldn't make out his features.

He advanced towards me, and I to him, his
Balding head was covered still with a mane of white hair,
Which shot out on all sides, like Ken Dodd,

And then it clicked – this was Stanley Chapman,
Of the Oulipo, Regent and President of the
London Institute of 'Pataphysics.

Incomparable Chapman, how I did rejoice
To see that you were not among the damned!
No greeting was left unsaid between us,

Then he asked: 'How long is it since you came
To the foot of the mount, across the boundless waters?'
'Jesus,' I replied, 'it seems like a long time ago,

But in truth, I came from the burning campus
Only this morning, I'm still in my first life,
But hope to gain a new life by this climb.'

When Chapman and Ginsberg heard my words,
They both stepped backwards suddenly, amazed,
Hardly able to believe their own ears.

One turned to Berrigan, the other one
Turned to a shade nearby: 'Paolo, get up,
This needs to be seen to be believed!'

He turned to me: 'Tell me, how are you doing,
Are you still in touch with the LIP, and with
The members of Oulipo, and more importantly,

Are you still writing and translating?
I still remember when we first met, in the Calder
Bookshop, you'd just published your translation

Of Queneau's *Elementary Morality*.'
'I joined the LIP soon afterwards,' I said,
'But haven't seen much of them lately,

Though I saw Alastair fairly recently.
As for Oulipo I'm still in touch with them –
I've seen Ian a few times, who presented my

*Quennets* to them. And they've invited me
To come to one of their monthly meetings,
To talk about my work. I'll take them up on this

As soon as I get a free moment – hopefully
Later this year. I've a new book of poems
Based on cave art, which is pure Oulipo.'

'You should do it,' he said, 'it would be good
To have some input from this side of the channel,
Especially now that I'm out of the loop.'

These were his words, and they made me more
Determined than ever to make that trip
To Paris, as soon as I'd got off the mount.

My eyes were now drawn to the sky which
Had filled up with stars, more and brighter than
I had ever seen whilst stargazing on Earth.

Berrigan said: 'Poet, what are you staring at?'
And I answered him: 'Why, at all these stars that now
Fill the night sky – I have never seen so many.'

And he to me: 'There is no light pollution here,
As you are accustomed to on Earth. That's why
The stars shine so brightly. Look, by

The moon is Capricorn. To the right that's
Sagittarius. The "S" shape further to the left –
Do you see it? – that's Aquarius.'

But then Ginsberg grabbed my arm and said:
'Look, there are some intruders over there!' –
He pointed to the place he had spotted them,

And there, along the valley's open side,
We saw a couple of figures moving furtively
Through the grass, stopping from time to time to check

They weren't being followed. When they reached the bottom
They quickly unfolded two chairs and a table,
Trying to blend in with the campers, then

Took out a chess board, and began to play.
The pieces were moulded in the shape of missiles
And warheads, and as you looked more closely

You could make out the faces of the players.
One of them was wiry and bald with a passive
Yet determined expression, the other was fat

With a mop of jet-black hair, shaved at the sides.
'If you're in any doubt,' said Ginsberg,
'The one on the left's Putin, his friend is Kim Jong Un.

Don't worry, the Alp Angels have spotted them.'
I did not see, so I cannot describe,
How the Alp Angels got there so quickly –

They must have flown down the sides of the slope – but as
Soon as they appeared the intruders rose quietly,
Exchanging a few words, and were escorted out.

The shade who had drawn close to Chapman's side
When he called, did not for a moment
Take his eyes off me during the skirmish.

'May the torch that lights your upwards path find
In your feet enough strength to reach the top,'
He then began, 'you may not recognise me,

But Paolo Borsellino was my name – I was
Part of the Palermo Antimafia Pool,
Killed by a Mafia car bomb in the 90s.'

'Oh,' I replied, 'I have visited your city
Many times, working with refugees, who themselves
Are often victims of the Mafia,

Who seduce them with money and cars and guns.
Your Antimafia Pool is legendary.'
'Friend,' he said, 'if you know my city and have recent

News of those parts, tell me, I am eager to know.'
'There's not much more I can tell you, I'm afraid,
I'm still a tourist there, but much good work

Is being done with migrants, and the Mayor of
Palermo has welcomed them with open arms,
Against the tide of opinion in Europe.

How long that will last and what the future
Holds in store I can't tell, perhaps Palermo
Is a special case, it seems so open to outsiders.

But the Mafia haven't gone away,
You'll hardly be surprised to hear that,
And Berlusconi's making a comeback.'

'That man is a curse – he only came
Into politics to protect his own
Media Empire from prosecution.

He's like a revenant, a vampire, sucking the blood
Of a nation, hanging out with call girls half his age,
How many times will he come back from the dead?

But enough of that. If my city has
Been kind to you, long may it continue so.
And may the good opinion you have of it

Continue to grow, nailed hard into your brain.'

## CANTO IX

The moon now shone so brightly in the sky
That it was like a second dawn –
Those given to myth would say that Aurora,

The concubine of old Tithonus,
Was getting it on with the moon goddess.
We were all sitting on the grass, looking

Up at the stars – Chapman delineated
Scorpio with an outstretched finger – when
Ginsberg lit another spliff and passed it round.

'This is finest Moroccan,' he said,
'I got it from Burroughs. When the moon's so high
It's only right that we should be so too.'

Three tokes and I was out for the count –
Sleep took me, stretched out on the grass
On which all five of us were sitting.

At the hour, close to dawn, when the swallow
Begins her melancholy lay,
Perhaps remembering her ancient woe,

And when our minds, released from the weight
Of the body, as from the practicalities
Of the day, become almost visionary,

I dreamed I had suffered a cardiac arrest,
Provoked by Burroughs' A-grade weed.
At once, Borsellino was on his mobile,

Calling Mountain Rescue to the scene –
Like a sea eagle, with wings outstretched,
Ready to swoop down from the sky,

A helicopter came, the noise of its blades
Filling the glade, then it settled on the ground.
At once, they put me on a stretcher,

As Ginsberg stubbed out the joint with his toe,
Then flew me off to A&E, whether to
Chelmsford or to Colchester I could not say.

When we got there the building was burning,
Smoke filled the air for miles about,
And as we tried to land it seemed that

The helicopter and I both burned.
The heat of that imaginary blaze
Was so intense it woke me from my sleep.

Just as Achilles awoke, startled –
Glancing around suspiciously,
Unsure where he now found himself –

When his mother whisked him off in her arms
Still sleeping from Chiron's care to Scyros,
Where the Greeks would later find him,

So I started, as soon as sleep left my eyes,
And turned pale, as one who is chilled with fear.
Beside me stood Berrigan, all alone, smoking a

Chesterfield. The sun was already risen
In the sky, and my face was turned towards the sea.
'Don't be afraid,' he said, 'you're doing fine.

Now, take a sip of this, it'll give you strength.'
He handed me some tea, from a flask,
And a couple of ginger biscuits.

'Take a look around,' he said, 'we're at rehab now.
There's the security wall that encircles it,
And up ahead, if you can see that cleft,

That's the gate. I'm afraid you got a bit stoned,
And passed out. We were a bit worried about you –
That gear from Burroughs sure packs a punch –

So Borsellino called St John's Ambulance,
And they drove you up here where it's warmer.
Ginsberg and the other shades remained below,

But Allen gave me this signed copy of *Howl*
For you to remember him by. If you don't
Want it, I'd be happy to hang on to it myself!'

As one who, first puzzled, becomes reassured,
And feels his fear slowly replaced by confidence,
Once things have been explained to him –

Such was the change in me. And when Berrigan saw me
Relax, my guide made his way slowly up and
Along the high bank with me following behind.

Reader, you see how lofty my theme grows!
Don't be surprised, then, if I pull the stops out now.
Close to the top, we reached a point from where

I could make out a metal turnstile,
With a small hut beside it (it was
Painted the same colour as the rock),

And leading up to it were three giant steps,
Carved in the rock, each one a different shade,
And peering out of the rock I saw a silent figure.

I slowly raised my eyes as he came
Out onto the topmost step – the brightness there
Was too much for my eyes, and I looked away.

I noticed that in his hand he held a dagger,
And as in the beach scene in Camus' *L'Étranger*,
So dazzling was the light reflected from it,

Each time I tried to look I could barely see.
I was beginning to wonder if this figure was
Not part of some Mountain Mafia, taking

Advantage of the isolation of this spot
To extort money from those who passed,
And that he might mean us harm. Then he

Called out to us: 'Stop right there strangers,
And speak from where you are, I'm not deaf.
What is it that you want? And where's your guide?

Have you come all this way by yourselves?
Who gave you the right to come here? Be careful,
You may live to regret making this journey.'

'Just this morning, a team from St John's Ambulance
Brought us up here from the terrace below,' said my guide.
'They pointed to the gate and told us to go there.'

'Was one of them Lucy?' he asked. 'A blonde.'
'That's right,' said Berrigan, 'and the driver
Looked like George Bernard Shaw, big red beard.'

'OK,' said the gatekeeper, softening, 'I'll take your word for it,
But we can't be too careful up here, we get
All sorts, and some people try to get in by force.'

We walked forward then, towards the steps.
The first was of white marble, so polished and smooth
That I saw myself reflected as I was

And saw that I was in bad need of a shave.
The second was black and blue, like a bruise,
With cracks and fissures across its surface,

As if it had been subjected to a great heat.
The third and topmost was of a red as deep
As blood that spurts from an artery.

The gatekeeper stood on this blood-red step,
His feet planted firmly on the ground.
Berrigan pushed me towards him, whispering:

'You've read Kafka, don't make the same mistake
As that loser in "Before the Law", ask him
Now, as politely as you can, to open the gate.'

I was tired. I stumbled. I found myself
Kneeling at his feet, like a supplicant, then
Looked up into his face and asked to be let in.

'Don't worry,' he said, 'the gate should open
If you're *bona fide*. But first, did they
Give you a card to get stamped at the Visitors'

Centre? It's got a Puffin logo on the front.'
Forgetting where I'd put it, I had to rummage around
In my rucksack, but eventually produced the card,

A little rumpled. 'OK,' he said, 'I'm going to
Give you your first stamp. Keep this card with you on
The journey up, and be sure to get it stamped at each terrace,

They'll want to see it if you get to the top.'
He reached behind the door of the hut for
The keys – one of them was a small silver

Yale key, the other was larger, and gold,
It looked like the sort of thing that would open
Up the gatehouse of some medieval castle.

'This fancy one,' he said, 'is just for show.
It's the little one that does the job, there's
A knack to it, you need to turn it gently,

While exerting pressure on the gate.' As he spoke,
We heard a click, then as he pushed on the
Turnstile it began to give slowly.

'There you go,' he said to us, 'enter, but
First, be warned, if you look back you'll have to
Come straight out again, don't ask, those are the rules.'

And then the pivots of that sacred turnstile,
Fashioned from wrought iron, heavy with rust,
Turned slowly in their sockets. The grating sound

Was louder and more stubborn than Tarpeia's
Treasury, when it was robbed by Caesar, and
As the whining pivots turned, I too turned,

For I heard voices chanting: '*I'm gonna*
*Go up to the spirit in the sky!*' –
Accompanied by the strange notes of that turnstile.

The clash of sounds made me remember what
It's like to listen to a rock band in Colchester
Arts Centre, when the PA mangles the vocals:

Sometimes you catch the words, sometimes you don't.

## CANTO X

When we had passed through the gate that remains
Forever shut to souls who think only of self,
And make the crooked way seem straight,

I heard it lock fast again, with a clunk;
My instincts made me want to look back,
                    but I checked myself, just in time.

We found ourselves
                              mounting a narrow cleft
In the rock, which kept

                              undulating from side to side
And up and down,
               like a wave that swells and pulls back,

When Berrigan, my guide, began: 'Careful,
You don't want to lose your footing, move with the walls,
Hugging the side that appears to pull back.

This may look like rock to you, but it has the properties
Of rubber, it's what the architects of this island
Call FRS – Flexible Rock Substitute.

It's one of the security features, designed to
Arrest the progress of those who come through the turnstile
Uninvited – though you'd think they could switch it off

For the likes of us. Let's go, it's making me feel queasy.'
The turbulent motion of the FRS
Forced us into taking ever smaller steps,

So that the already waning moon had sunk
Completely out of sight before we were
Finally squeezed out of that rubber vagina.

But when we were free of its grip at last, and
Emerged once more into the open air
Where the high mountain towered above us,

Both tired out and uncertain of our way
We stopped for a breather on a level shelf,
Lonelier than are roads through war-torn wastes.

From the edge which is the edge of emptiness
To the foot of the perpendicular rock face, there was
Space for three coffins laid end to end.

As far as I could see, looking ahead,
Both to my left and to my right,
The ledge did not vary in its width,

And standing there, getting our breath back,
I noticed that all the inner cliff,
Which, rising sheer, offered no foothold to the climber,

Was covered all over with intricate carvings. 'These,'
Said Berrigan, 'according to the Guidebook, were
Executed by the Artist-in-Residence,

Grayson Perry, cut into the raw rock face with lasers.'
The rock was so cluttered with carvings that at
First it was difficult to make them out,

But as I looked more closely, individual scenes
Emerged from the tangled imbroglio.
There was a scene outside a country home,

Where an old man with a walker made circuits
Of his house, that in its expert execution
Recreated the effects of slow movement.

From the medals on his chest I saw now that this
Was Captain Tom Moore, who raised money for
The NHS before his 100th birthday. Beneath,

A text read: 'I never thought I'd raise so much!'
Another scene, close by, showed Captain Tom
Meeting the Queen, humbled by the encounter.

Then beside this another image showed Captain Tom
Lying in a hospital bed, with an oxygen mask, dying
From Covid-19. A nurse sat at his side, weeping.

'Why don't you look at the other parts as well?'
Said Berrigan, who pressed close to my side.
And so I turned my eyes, and looked ahead,

Past the nurse's crouched form to the place he was
Pointing at, where I saw other scenes cut in the rock.
Stepping in front of Berrigan, I drew near the cliff

So that my eyes could take it all in.
Carved in the sheer face of the rock I saw
Depicted there a Hell's Angel with *Death or Glory*

Tattooed on his arm, who had pulled up his
Harley onto the pavement to help an old
Lady who had fallen off her mobility scooter;

I saw the CEO of a big city bank
Handing back his bonus, and a rock star
Who was unstrapping his guitar

To hand it over to one of his fans from the crowd,
Who proceeded to improvise an impromptu solo;
And above him there was a footballer –

Was it David Beckham? – who was kicking
A ball around with a group of laughing
Boys in an African refugee camp;

Then a little further on I saw President
Obama at the funeral service for the
Reverend Clementa Pinckney, one of the nine

Killed by Dylann Roof in the Charleston
Massacre, singing 'Amazing Grace' with the
Whole congregation, testing my senses,

One of which said, 'No,' while the other said,
'Yes, they truly sing!' With equal art
The tears which some wiped from their eyes

Were traced so faithfully that you would
Have sworn the rock had turned to water.
I shifted off from that spot to observe

More closely other stories likewise lasered
In the rock beyond the face of Obama.
I made out clearly the face and hands of

Pope Francis, Bishop of the Slums, washing
The feet of kids hooked on paco; I saw
Nelson Mandela ushering a chambermaid out of

His hotel room as he bent to make his own bed;
And close by I saw depicted the story of
José 'Pepe' Mujica, President of Uruguay,

Who, when elected president in 2009,
Donated 90% of his salary to charity,
And ditched the presidential palace,

To live on a ramshackle farm with his wife.
As I stood there gawping at these jostling
Humilities, and wondering at the artistry,

'Look, over there, how slowly they approach,
That crowd of spirits,' whispered Berrigan,
'They will show us the way to the stairs.'

My eyes, caught up in their wonderment,
Were eager for new sights, so I
Was not slow to turn them towards him.

Reader, when you see how these spirits pay
Their debts, don't lose heart, even if
The punishment seems harsh. Remember,

This is not like Hell where the torment never
Stops – here the spirits are all intent on
Finding a better way, building a better world.

'Master, the shapes I see lumbering towards us
There,' I said, 'don't look like spirits at all.
I don't know what to make of them – they look

More like some kind of care robots, or androids.'
And Berrigan answered me: 'The grievous nature
Of their punishment bends their bodies down to the ground –

At first I wasn't sure what to make of them myself.
Concentrate, and try to disentangle with your eye
What moves beneath those heavy loads –

Can you see now how each one beats his breast?'
Oh stupid brains, happy to puff up your egos
Endlessly by massaging your credit ratings,

Pouring your energies blindly into the pursuit of
Accumulating smart gadgets and consumer goods
And cars too big to even fit on the roads,

Do you not understand that alone we remain like larvae,
But that together we could be butterflies
That soar into the air in clouds of light?

Why do your pretensions have no ceiling?
Why does your ambition never stop to look about?
Why do you not see the damage that you cause?

Every smart phone you upgrade leaves behind it
A trail which leads to a war in the Congo
Or a toxic sulphur lake in Mongolia.

How can you even look yourselves in
The mirror,
                    stuck in your larval form like worms?

Sometimes, in a country church, one sees a corbel
Carved in human form taking the weight of the high roof,
Its chest crushed tightly down against its knees,

And so lifelike is this *jeu d'esprit* that
It can cause physical discomfort in
Even the most casual churchgoer.

This is how those souls appeared and how they
Made me feel, crushed as they were like salesmen under the
Weight of the washing-machines that straddled their backs.

True, some of them were more compressed, some less,
Depending on the specifications of the appliance that
Pressed on each one's back, but even the most patient

Of them all seemed through tears to say : 'I can't go on.'

## CANTO XI

'Our first mover, who relates to another in a
Way mirroring the relationship of father and child,
Living as resident in the revolving spherical

Shells in which, according to ancient
Astronomy, the celestial bodies are set,
Not forced by imposed stricture there to live

But freely choosing so to reside because of your
Undying affection for your first creation, those spiritual
Beings usually depicted as being winged,

Venerated be the name designating your person,
Venerated the authority and influence you have
Over others, over all created beings, for it is

Appropriate to the situation to make our expressions
Of gratitude to your animating principle
Inducing that one of the four basic taste sensations

Typically triggered by sucrose. Let the state
Of tranquillity of the sphere in which you hold a
Pre-eminent position move towards us, for we

Cannot reach it by motion, growth or effort of our own,
If it does not move towards us, even with all the
Mental and physical resources at our disposal.

And as those spiritual beings usually depicted as
Being winged give up or lose their mental powers by
Which they control their wishes and intentions to you,

Uttering Hosannahs in musical notes with
Inflections and modulations, so let the members
Of the family of biped primate mammals anatomically

Related to the apes but distinguished by
Greater brain development and a capacity for
Articulated speech and abstract thought give up theirs.

Give us on this solar day of twenty-four hours
Beginning at midnight our daily sustenance – as you
Miraculously gave it to the Israelites in their journey

Through the wilderness, without which in this unduly
Exacting region uninhabited by members of the
Family of biped primate mammals anatomically

Related to the apes but distinguished by
Greater brain development and a capacity for thought,
He goes backwards who most strives to advance.

And as we cease to resent all others for the
Acts causing discomfort or offence that we have
Been forced to endure, so do you cease to resent

Us in a manner showing devotion and tenderness,
And do not regard too closely our undeserving
Moral or personal merit or demerit. Our capacity for endurance

Or exertion, which is conquered and brought into
Subjection without difficulty, do not entice to evil
By promise of pleasure or gain from the ancient adversary,

But set it at liberty from this ancient one who
Would turn us from the right path by pricking us with
Sharp pointed metal accoutrements usually

Used to encourage the forwards and rapid movements
Of domesticated quadruped equine mammals.
This last petition to your being, oh dear one who has

Power and authority over others, we do not make
For our own individual selves, since there is no need,
But for those beings who have stayed or remained at our rear.'

So, praying with heavy words for others' wellbeing,
Those souls moved slowly beneath the weight of their
Washing-machines, like creatures we might meet in a dream,

Or in a painting by Hieronymus Bosch reworked by
Magritte. They were not equally tormented by their loads,
For while some lugged Bosch Titans and Hotpoints

Others carried smaller machines, Zanussi Compacts
And Candy Aquas, going around and around on the
First ledge, washing away the filth of the world.

If these souls, up here, pray so zealously for our good,
Think what we down here can do for them,
If we only think of them from time to time.

We ought, indeed, to help them wash away the stains
And the dirt they have picked up here on Earth,
Like careless children playing in the mud, so that they

May emerge in blue whiteness amidst the wheeling stars.
'I've seen showroom scrambles on Black Friday,'
Said Berrigan, my guide, 'but this is something else.

Where's the manager here? If the customer's still got
Any rights at all, someone should take pity on you
And free you from your loads, so you can stand up

And give us a hand. Can someone here show us the way
To reach the stairs, and if there are several paths,
Tell us which one is the shortest and the least steep?

This man who travels at my side bears his own weight –
He still carries the body he was born with on Earth
And so, against his will, is slow to climb.'

A few words were muttered in response to Berrigan's
Bantering – I'm not sure they all appreciated his jokes –
But it was unclear to me who spoke them.

Then someone piped up, saying: 'Come with us,
Along this bank to the right, and you will find
A path a living person can easily climb.

If I were not weighed down by this Bosch
That presses down on my proud neck, so that
I must keep my eyes glued to the ground,

I would look up at this unnamed man
Who is still living, and see if he recognises my face
So that he may take pity on my burdened back.

I was born in Edinburgh, where I was adopted
At four months by Labour supporters from Aberdeen.
Gove is my name, perhaps you've heard it before?

I started off in the state sector, but quickly won
A scholarship to Robert Gordon College, then read English,
When it *was* still *English*, at Lady Margaret Hall.

My achievements, I confess it here, made me arrogant,
And I held all men, and women actually, in such disdain that
I became incapable of listening to anyone but myself.

Many suffered because of my decisions in
Office, as any child in a state school in England
Could tell you. I took pride in taking soft subjects

Off the curriculum and replacing them with Grammar.
I took pride in the hard-lined example I set, which led
Gavin to reopen schools prematurely in the pandemic.

Pride didn't just ruin me, but all my party, dragging them
With it from calamity to calamity until we delivered Brexit.
And once we'd achieved this calamitous goal we were

So wrapped up in our success that we didn't even notice we
Were in the epicentre of a global pandemic until it was too late.
The weight which I refused to bear when alive

I am now forced to bear among the dead
Until my back has felt the pain it inflicted
On others down on Earth – I'm here for the long haul.'

I had my head bent down to the ground, to hear his
Grating words, when someone – not he who spoke –
Twisted around beneath a Siemens Avantgarde,

And straining to recognise my face, he called out to me,
Pushing against the weight of his machine to keep
His eyes on me, as I walked bent down amidst those souls.

'Oh my God!' I said, 'aren't you Damien Hirst,
Pride of Bristol, who did the shark in formaldehyde,
And reinvented the art of spin painting?'

'The works that Rachel Whiteread casts,'
He said, 'shine more radiantly now;
Hers is the honour today – mine is far less.

I wouldn't have been so generous to her,
I must admit, while I was still down on Earth,
That would have been career suicide –

You don't rise to pre-eminence in the art world
By promoting your competitors. But for such
Arrogance the price is paid here – I've swapped

My spin paintings for this spinning drum I carry.
I wouldn't even be here, were it not that,
While I still had the means, I set up a charity,

Strummerville, to help young musicians,
After the death of Joe Strummer in 2002.
How up themselves people are in the art world,

It makes me sick, and how short a time fame lasts,
Unless some generation of fuckwits follows!
Once Emin held centre stage in the

Media; Perry now is all the rage,
Dimming the lustre of the other's fame.
So, in the book world, one Gilbert Adair

Takes pre-eminence from the other,
One Smith wins the prizes while the other
Goes out of fashion; and already making a splash

At the book fairs is a young gun who'll drive
All of these writers out of the limelight.
Commercial success is just a gust of wind,

It blows about, now here now there, and as
It changes direction it changes name.
Were you to reach a ripe old age like Beckett,

Or die screaming in your crib like Chatterton,
Would it make any difference a thousand years from now?
And what are ten centuries to eternity?

Less than the blinking of an eye in the
Context of the geological
time span of the planet.

You see that soul ahead crawling along under
The weight of that giant twin-tub? All the
TV channels once resounded with his name,

Now it's hardly whispered in London, where he
Was once Mayor, before his mad ambition
Made him turn Brexiteer – once so proud,

But, now, become as venal as a pimp.
Your earthly fame is like the green grass
On a fairway; it comes and goes, and the

Chemicals that make it grow from the soil
Are the same ones that make it wither and fade.'
And I to him: 'Your words ring true, friend, they remind

Me of what Lyotard says about postmodernism,
And they make me wonder about my own ambitions, too,
But tell me, who's the one you spoke about just now?'

'That's Boris Johnson,' he replied, 'and he is here
Because he treated Brexit and moving into number 10
Like nothing more than his next career opportunities,

Without stopping for a moment to think. So puffed up with
Pride was he when he was elected into office that he
Dismissed the threat of Covid-19 with a swish of his hand,

And from that moment one calamity was quickly followed
By another: he locked down too late, failed to protect care homes,
Failed to supply PPE to the NHS, failed to introduce testing

Quickly enough for it to have any meaningful effect, failed to
Introduce an effective system of Test and Trace, and failed to
Dismiss his Chief Advisor when he broke lockdown rules,

Inaugurating a free-for-all culminating in thousands of
People descending on Bournemouth beach, which helped ensure
The UK had more deaths per capita than any other nation on Earth.

So he crawls around and has crawled since his soul died,
Knowing no rest. Such coin is paid up here
By those who were up themselves down there.'

And I: 'If it is true that any soul
Who has put off good deeds till the very end
Must wait down below before they can ascend,

Then how come he's got up here so fast?'
'You may well ask,' he said, 'not
Much good can be said of this man.

He's a liar, an opportunist and a serial
Adulterer, he fucked us over with Brexit,
And messed up on Covid-19, as I've said,

And then he was the worst Foreign Secretary
In living memory: it was his careless words
That caused Nazanin Zaghari-Ratcliffe

To be shut up in Tehran's Evin Prison.
And when he had a chance to right the wrong
He had done in Iran, he said nothing.

His pride stopped him, for he is a man who
Can never admit he has made a mistake,
A sorry inheritance from his father.

And yet, in the fight against Covid-19,
Amidst his serial blunders, he did one good thing,
In backing then rolling out the vaccine.

It was this act that sped him here.'

## CANTO XII

Side by side, like oxen under a yoke, as you
Can still see in rural Vietnam, we shuffled along,
That burdened artist and I, as long as Berrigan

Permitted, but when he said: 'Let's move on, it's time to
Give your friend a break, for each one here must fly his own kite,'
I stood upright again, to walk the way men were born to,

But though my body was upright, my thoughts,
Perplexed, remained bowed down to the earth.
'Surely,' I asked, 'some of these souls, like Gove,

Are still among the living – what are they doing here?'
'Ah!' said Berrigan, 'Remember what I said earlier,
About worlds in parallel, some of these souls here

Are dead, some of them are just spiritually dead,
And their real bodies still go about their business on Earth,
Without realising they have a second existence up here.

And again, a few of the spirits you'll meet here are still among
The good of the Earth, but here they steal a march on the crowd.'
'One more thing, if I may,' I said then, and Berrigan with a nod

Encouraged me to go on. 'This Covid-19 everyone's talking
About. How come it's still a worry on this island – I mean,
Everyone here's dead already.' And Berrigan replied:

'That's a common misconception – but take it from me, the
Living die from life into death, but the dead can still die again, from
One death to another.' Now, I was moving more quickly once more,

Following the footsteps of Berrigan, my guide,
Both of us showing what mountaineers we had become,
When, 'Now, look down,' said the poet, 'you'll dig it,

And it will make your journey pass more quickly,
To see on what ground you put your feet.'
As tombs of the dead set in a church floor

Often bear carved likenesses of the deceased,
To show us how they appeared when still alive,
Images that still have the power to move us to tears,

Just so, I saw – but far more exuberantly
Portrayed, for this was the work of the mountain's
Turner-Prize winning Artist-in-Residence –

Stone carvings there, etched by laser like the art
We had seen carved into the cliff face, covering
The path that juts out from the mountainside.

My eyes looked down on he who was once supposed
To be the noblest creature of all creation,
Now bald and red-faced and wrinkled like a toad.

My eyes looked down on Gilbert and George, cocksure of
Their own pre-eminence in the history of art,
One with a cock in his mouth, one with a cock in his arse.

My eyes looked down on the face of Liam Brady,
Unrepentant till the end over the children he
Had tortured and murdered and buried on the moor.

My eyes looked down on the sad face of Chris Huhne, once
So proud, now forced to resign over a speeding case
Where his wife had falsely claimed to be driving.

And Margaret Thatcher, I saw your picture there, one
Who had once trodden on the miners and the hunger
Strikers, now trodden underfoot by all who pass.

Arachne too, crazed, I saw in her spider form,
Hanging by a thread above her perfect tapestry, which
Had caused the goddess Athene to fly into such a rage.

And Nigella Lawson, I saw your beautiful face there,
The domestic goddess, reduced to tears
By the man you had turned to in your grief.

And Martin Amis, I saw your fat face there
Looking down your nose at the world that surrounds you
Which you plumped up then fed to your baggy monsters.

Nigel Farage I saw then, gloating over the Brexit vote,
Then disappearing from sight, leaving others to sort out
The mess created by his xenophobic zeal.

Next, I saw the chastened face of that vile Holocaust
Denier, I will not soil these pages with his name,
His respectability torn to shreds in open court.

Now, I saw the publicist, Max Clifford,
Jailed for sexually abusing his victims,
Keeling over from a heart attack in his prison cell.

Now, I saw the computer tycoon, Tim Rakewell,
Lying dead in the road after his fatal car accident,
As the ambulance arrived to clear up the mess.

My eyes beheld the once great city of Mosul,
Ah! To think you were once the proud city of Nineveh!
Now reduced to ashes by ISIS and coalition forces.

What other brush could paint, or video artist film
Such lineaments and shadings? At such skill
The subtlest genius would have stared in awe.

The dead seemed dead, the living alive. An eyewitness
To the events themselves could not have seen them better
Than did I, who trod upon them, head bent low.

Oh stupid brains, with your big ideas,
Heads stuck up your own arses with your pride!
Why do you never look down at the road of shit you tread?

By now, we had advanced further round the mount,
And a greater part of the sun's orbit had been completed
Than I, caught up in my wonder, would have guessed,

When Berrigan, who always kept his eyes open
As we trecked on, said: 'Now lift up your head, poet,
You have spent enough time lost in your dreaming,

Look up ahead, there's one of the Alp Angels,
Making ready to greet us, and put us on the right path.
By the fresh look on his face he must just be

Starting his shift. Look sharp, and give him a smile,
So that he won't think twice about helping us up.
Remember, you won't get a second bite at the cherry!'

By this stage of our journey I was used to him
Admonishing me, and telling me to hurry up,
So I didn't let what he said get me down.

The elderly guide came up to us, clothed
In his gleaming white uniform, and in his face,
Despite his years, was something of the trembling of a morning star.

He beckoned with his arms, then turned to lead the way,
So that we saw clearly the winged logo of the
Alp Angels on the back of his sweatshirt.

'Come,' he said, 'the steps are just over here,
You'll find that they are easy to climb.
Not that many climbers come up by this way,

But those who do are always glad to reach these steps.'
Then he stopped for a moment and asked me for my card,
Which I slipped out of my pocket. He took out

A rubber stamp, then stamped my card with a P,
Then, handing it back, he said: 'Don't lose it,
You may have need of it further up.' He led

Us to where the rock was cut out, where
He stopped suddenly, so that I walked straight into his
Back, glancing my cheek against the wings on his

Sweatshirt, then he wished us a safe journey.
As, on the way up to the mountain top
Crowned by the monastery of Skellig Michael,

On the Skellig islands off the coast
Of Ireland, that well-governed nation,
The difficulty of the steep ascent is eased

By steps carved out of rock on the hillside,
So here, the steep bank that leads to the second
Terrace has been made easier with steps,

Though, on both sides, the high rock presses close.
While we walked towards those steps, the song
'No Woman, No Cry' rang out from loudspeakers embedded in

The rock, more sweetly than I can describe.
How different these passageways to those of Hell! Here, one
Enters to music, there to grief-stricken wailings.

As we were making our way up the carved steps
I noticed I suddenly felt more agile, and lighter,
Than I had felt before on level ground.

'Berrigan,' I said, 'tell me, what's come over me?
I suddenly feel as if I could keep climbing all day.'
He answered: 'When the P's that still remain

To be stamped in your book have all been added,
And you have collected the complete set,
Then will your feet be lighter still.

They will no longer feel the hard road
But will rejoice as they are urged to climb.
It's the same with those pilgrims on the road to

Santiago de Compostela – the more scallops
They accumulate the better they walk.'
Then I did something anyone might do when in high

Spirits, but which I hadn't managed since the days I was
At primary school – I took a run up the steps,
Then stopped suddenly, and without losing the energy

Of my momentum, rather preserving it as in a
Coiled spring, flipped backwards, performing a somersault
In mid-air like Joe Wicks, landing on my feet with only the slightest

Wobble. Observing this, Berrigan smiled at me.

## CANTO XIII

We were now standing at the top of the steps,
And for a second time we reached a smooth ledge,
Where the hill that heals those who climb had been cut away.

There a terrace encircles the mountain, just
Like the one below, except that this one
Bends more sharply. The place was deserted,

Nor were there any carvings to be seen.
The cliff face was bare, and in parts hidden
By scaffolding which rattled in the wind,

The roadway too was bare, its rock a livid hue.
'If we stand here until someone shows up
To give us directions,' said Berrigan,

'We could be in for a long wait.' Then,
Staring straight up at the sun, Berrigan
Raised his arms as if in supplication,

Turning his body round to face the sun's warmth.
'Oh cherished light, that lovers curse,
You shine on the jungle, on the tundra,

The sea, the ghetto, and on this barren height.
Not everyone can look up at you like this,
It hurts their eyes, and it is hurting mine,

As I call to you. You warm the world, you
Shed your light on it, unless there's a solar eclipse,
Your radiant light should always be our guide!'

We had already walked along that ledge
For a good country mile as they say in Essex,
Moving easily in the warmth of the sun,

When all of a sudden we heard voices fill the air.
We could not see where they came from, and I
Looked about in vain to see if they were

Spirits concealed in the fissures of the rock.
The first voice that came flying past us called
Out loud and clear: 'Open your doors to refugees!'

And then carried on behind us, the words echoing.
And then, before it faded quite,
Another voice cried out: '*I'm* Spartacus!'

Then that voice too sped by. 'Berrigan,' I asked,
'What voices are these?' And as I spoke there came
A third, saying: 'Love those by whom you suffer harm!'

Berrigan began leafing through the pages of
The Guidebook, then said: 'It explains it all here.
It looks like we're in the place where the Envious are

Punished, if that's the right word, and perhaps it is, for it
Says here this is the "Whip of Envy". I think the idea
Is that these voices set a good example, helping you

Overcome your envy: kind of "Love your neighbour"
Rather than "Why's that geek got a bigger car than me?"
The first voice, it says, is that of the British artist Sarah Wood,

Whose films about migration encourage
A progressive outlook. The second is from
The life of Spartacus – you may have seen

The film with Charlton Heston. That last voice
Was the Dalai Lama, who says likewise "In the practice
Of tolerance, one's enemy is the best teacher."

Later on, it says, we'll encounter the "Curb of Envy" –
We should hear that before we reach the Pass of Pardon,
Which is the name it gives to the next set of steps.

Now, take a look up ahead, look closely
And you'll see some spirits over there,
All of them huddled up against the cliff.'

I looked ahead, straining my eyes, and saw
A group of souls dressed in dark cagouls with hoods,
Exactly the same livid colour as the rock.

As we drew closer I heard their prayers and cries:
Some prayed to God, some to the Buddha, some
Chanted like followers of Hare Krishna,

While others just cried out for their mothers.
I can't believe that anyone who walks the Earth
Today could be so hard-hearted that they would not

Have been pierced by pity at the sight I now saw:
When I got close enough to see the nature of
Their torment, the sight pressed bitter tears from my eyes.

Their hoods were pulled down over their faces,
And each one's head was glued to another's shoulder,
The wall of the cliff supporting their bodies.

They brought to mind Bruegel's vast canvas, hanging
In Naples, *The Parable of the Blind*,
Where one man leads the other,

Stirring up pity and terror in the onlooker,
Not only by the forlorn expressions on their faces
But by their blank looks which plead better than words.

And just as the blind cannot profit from the sun,
So the shades that I speak of now
Were shut off from the light of the heavens:

The eyes of these spirits had been stapled shut
As in some ghastly horror movie, where
Some deranged psychopath gets his kicks by

Prolonging the agony of his victims.
I felt ashamed to be standing there gawping,
Staring wide-eyed at shades who could not stare back.

I turned to Berrigan, my guide, who knew
At once what I wished to ask. 'Speak,' he said,
'But make your words brief and to the point.'

Berrigan was walking to one side of me,
Close to the edge of the terrace, where one misplaced
Footstep could easily lead to a fall

(For there was no safety rail on these heights),
While on the other side were gathered those souls
Whose tears seeped out through the rusting staples.

I turned towards them and said: 'Dear souls, assured
That one day you will see the exalted light again,
Which is now the only object of your desire,

May the powers of this mountain wash away the murk
Clouding your minds, that the stream of memory
May flow through them with renewed clarity,

Tell me, for I would be glad to know it,
Whether any among you come from Ireland,
Where I was born, or from England, where I have lived.'

'Brother, each one of us is now a citizen of
This one true state. But you will find here some
Who once passed through the lands you mention.'

This haughty answer to my question seemed to come
From a little ahead of where I stood, so I moved on
To where these souls could hear me speak clearly.

Among the others I saw one shade which looked
Expectant, holding its chin out as the blind do. 'Spirit,'
I said, 'preparing yourself to climb,

If it was you who spoke just now, tell me
Your name, and where you lived while on Earth,
And why you suffer here as you do.'

'I was not from the lands you mention, I'm a Scot,
From Edinburgh. I was raised by Jehovah's
Witnesses, but grew up to hate that creed.

Though my name is Sue Wise, wise I was not.
It always gave me joy to witness others
In misfortune, whether stuck in traffic

Or stuck in a bad relationship, enjoying
That more than my own achievements.
If you don't believe me, listen now,

And you will see how far I went in my madness.
I was already approaching retirement,
When a surprise QAA Inspection was announced.

My colleagues at the university were
Quietly confident, but when the inspectors
Arrived it was a disaster from the word go.

The students, who'd been primed in advance,
Didn't show, the Head of Department's car broke down,
And the PowerPoint didn't work.

I revelled in their humiliation, as the
Chief Inspector wrote out his damaging report,
Putting the Department into Special Measures.

I was seized with a surge of joy so fierce
That I raised my clenched fists to the heavens and shouted:
"Maybe there's a God up there after all!"

I did not seek my peace with God or with
My family till my final years – turning
Back at the last to the truth I had once spurned.

And even so, repentance would not have reduced
My debt had not Peter Pettinaio
Of the Watch Tower Society

Annulled my previous disfellowshipping,
And remembered me in all his prayers.
But who are you, so keen to find out about

Us here, who walk with your eyes wide open,
Or so it seems to me, breathing as you speak?'
'My eyes,' I said, 'may yet be taken from me

In this place, though only for a short while –
They have not been given overmuch to envy, for
I was more one to celebrate the success of friends.

I'm more worried about the torments in
The circle below where I feel the weight
Already – for no poet is without his pride.'

Then she asked, puzzled: 'Who has brought you up
Here to us, if you plan on returning down below?'
And I: 'The one who is with me but does not speak.

I am still of the living. And if you
Want me to, I would be glad to run an
Errand on your behalf back on Earth.'

'Oh, this is such a strange thing to hear,' she
Answered, 'it's a sure sign that God loves you.
Yes, help me with a prayer from time to time,

And I beg you, by all you hold most dear,
If ever you set foot in Lothian
Restore my good name among my family there.

You'll find them amongst those thrifty dreamers who were
Stupid enough to dig up their streets for a tramway,
Putting the city in debt for 30 years –

But still, the taxi drivers will lose out the most.'

## CANTO XIV

'Who's this fancy pants roaming round our shelf,
Before his soul has been set free by Death,
Opening and closing his eyes at will?'

'I haven't the foggiest. All I know is he's not
Alone, there's more than one pair of boots on this catwalk.
Why don't you pop the question, you're closer, and speak nicely,

As you would at a show, to make sure you get a reply.'
There to my right I overheard two spirits gassing away
Their heads bent together like conspirators,

Then all of a sudden they raised their faces up as if
To address me, and one said, clearing his throat:
'Dear soul, who still dwelling in your mortal body

Foot this hill, please let us know where you
Hale from, and who you are, for this is
Something that has never happened before.'

And I replied: 'Between County Down and
County Antrim there winds a stream that rises
Near the summit of Slieve Croob, its course is

More than fifty miles from start to finish.
From along its banks I bring this body –
There's no point telling you my name,

For on Earth I am a poet.' 'If I've caught the
Gist of what you're saying,' replied the shade,
'You're talking about the Lagan, am I right?'

The other said to him: 'If he's talking about
The Lagan, why on Earth would he beat about
The bush like this, to avoid saying its name,

As if it were something too awful to pronounce?'
And the shade who had been questioned replied:
'No idea, but he says he's a poet, and poets are wordy,

But it's fitting that the name of such a place perish,
For from its source, where the rugged mountain chain starts,
A place so stuffed with drinkers that few surpass it,

Down to the stinking estuary where it
Throws back the waters that the sky has carried
From the Irish Sea, virtue is spat upon.

Men run away from it as from a
Booby-trapped car. The place is cursed, to be sure,
Else its souls have become sectarian zombies.

Past Dromore where Ulster's very own Ku Klux Klan
Hatched its plots – the Orange Order to you –
This river first directs its puny course;

It keeps on dropping down past Blackskull,
Where racism is a badge of pride,
Disdainfully twisting away from this dishonoured spot,

Then, after descending through barren fields,
It finds Donaghcloney, where Loyalist
Paramilitaries colluded with rogue police officers

With no fear that the law would catch them.
Still further down it falls – the more this damned
And God-forsaken sewer expands the worse it gets –

It passes Mazetown, where sectarian
Violence was institutionalised, then
Reaches Lisburn, where "Big John" McMichael,

Commander of the Ulster Freedom Fighters,
Assassinated any Republicans unlucky
Enough to end up on his "shopping list".

I'm not done yet, matey, and you mark my words,
For it was another *Murphy* – yes, Lenny
Murphy of Belfast, leader of the Shankill

Butchers – who snatched Catholics off the
Streets in the 1970s to be beaten then
Tortured then hacked to death with butchers' knives.

The Troubles knows no greater monstrosities.'
As at the news of some fearful atrocity
Or disaster, the face of the listener

Displays the shock received just so that shade,
Intent on listening, revealed his consternation,
As he heard the other's words.

The words of the one, the other's face,
Made me so curious to know the pair,
That I asked them to reveal their names.

At this the shade who spoke to me at first
Replied: 'So, you expect me to do what
You refused to do for me? Well have it your way.

Gearalt Duffy used to be my name, and
You'll still find it on the label of my fashion range.
Jealousy was quick to boil up my blood,

Whenever I saw another designer triumph
On the catwalk, you'd see me turn green with envy.
I hated it when my new range wasn't the best.

I sowed this envy, now I reap this reward!
People are eejits to pin their hopes
Where partnership has no place.

And this is Rian, pride of the Murphys – once head
Of a Dublin Fashion House, without an heir who
Might inherit any of his fortune.

From Malahide to Dalkey, from Maynooth
To the sea, their house is not the only one
Stripped bare of all that has any worth.

For all the land within these boundaries,
And beyond, is choked by the corporate greed
Which has run through the city like a plague,

Tearing the very heart out of the place to
Feed the Celtic Tiger, driving out the bums,
The designers, the musicians and the artists alike.

Where is Synge? Where is Sean O'Casey?
Where is the incomparable Flann O'Brien?
Where is Thin Lizzy? Where is Boyzone?

When, in Dublin, will we see again
A Lady Gregory? When a Behan,
That consummate artist of the gutter?

Northerner, I can only weep when I
Remember that Samuel Beckett and James
Joyce lived among us once, and what about

William Butler Yeats, and his brother Jack,
Now there was a family, but who is there
Today to replace the likes of them will you tell me now?

Dublin city, why don't you just shut up shop?
Why don't you just slide beneath the snot-green
Sea in shame? Today your city walls

Can contain no more shit than they do already,
For they are crammed with corporate bullies,
With drug barons, and corrupt priests.

If the priests of Ireland were to drop dead tomorrow,
We would all be better off by a mile – although the record
Of their evil deeds would remain online for all to see.

Ah, Seamus Heaney, your legacy is safe, for
There's no chance it will be betrayed by bad poets –
Today Ireland has no poets at all.

But go now, Northerner, I would rather weep,
Much rather weep, than speak another word –
Our blathering has so wrung my sorrowing mind.'

We knew those good souls heard us move away,
And as they said nothing we felt sure of
Having taken the right path to climb.

As we were walking on our lonely road
There came, like lightning ripping through the air,
A voice, shot out at us from hidden speakers:

'*I'll be a fugitive, and whoever finds me will kill me!*' –
Then it rolled past like thunder dying down
After a sudden cloudburst.

Our ears had just begun recovering from this shock,
When the rumbling of a second voice came –
One clap of thunder following on another:

'*I am Aglauros who was turned to stone!*'
With that, instead of going on, I moved
A little closer to Berrigan.

'What was all that about?' I asked him.
'They're recorded voices,' he said, 'that are triggered
By our steps, they're meant to be a kind of warning,

I guess, look, here's what the Guidebook says:
"As you exit the second terrace you will
Hear dismembered voices in the air.

The first is that of Cain, who slew his brother
Through envy, the second is that of Aglauros,
Who, because she was envious of her sister,

The god Mercury turned to livid stone."
Do you get the message? Jealousy doesn't pay,
And if you give in to it, as Johnny Cash says,

"Sooner or later God'll cut you down."'

## CANTO XV

We were three hours from the first part of that
Canonical division of the day
That Monteverdi celebrates in his

*Vespro della Beata Vergine* of 1610 – in
Other words it was mid-afternoon on the Essex Alp,
As it is midnight here, where I am writing this.

Now, the late rays of the sun struck us bang
On the nose, for we had progressed so far
Round the mount that we were walking due west.

Then suddenly I felt my eyes dazzled by
A light far brighter than the afternoon sun –
I had no idea where it was coming from.

Instinctively, I placed both my hands over
My eyes to shield them from the glare, using them as
A visor to combat the intensity of the light,

Yet my precaution was of little use.
As a ray of light is bounced back from
Water or from glass, the angle of reflection

Equal to the angle of incidence,
As they teach you at school in the physics lab,
So that light was reflected from the smooth stone path

Right into my eyes from beneath, so that I had
To turn aside to shield myself from its brightness.
'Berrigan,' I said, 'what's going on? That light's

So bright I can barely see. And it feels
Like it's moving towards us. What do we do now?'
Calmly, Berrigan handed me some shades,

Then said: 'Don't fret, I'm pretty sure it's just
One of the Alp Angels coming to show
Us the way up. The lights are coming from

His jeep, and I'd guess from their brightness, that
He's got his fog lights on for some reason –
There must be some mountain mist up ahead.'

Berrigan had barely finished talking
When the jeep pulled over and turned off
Its headlights. For a moment the change was

So stark that everything seemed to go dark,
But when my eyes once more adjusted to
The natural light of the sun I could see

The Alp Angel making his way towards us, smiling.
'Sorry about the fog lights, guys,' he said,
'Visibility's poor up ahead, though it will

Be easier on foot as long as you tread carefully.
Come, this is the way to the stairs up,
You'll find them less steep by far than those below.'

We thanked him for his help, then he asked for
My card, adding a stamp before we split.
Already, we were beginning the ascent

When we heard voices and guitars from somewhere behind
Crying '*Have mercy, baby!*' and others, as if from
A different stage, singing '*The winner takes it all.*'

Then, as we moved away from this music,
Hoping to take advantage of our time alone,
I turned to Berrigan, my guide, to question him.

'What did the shade from Dublin mean,' I said, 'the one
Who called himself Duffy, when he spoke of those
Who pin their hopes where partnership has no place?'

'He knows the price tag attached to his worst fault,'
He answered, 'so it's only natural
That he should censure it. For in so far as

Your desires are fixated on things which are
Diminished by being shared, you are prone to envy.
But if you can only grasp that sharing

Is something that both enriches the giver
And the receiver, for it creates a community
Of ownership, then you are released from this trap.

And everyone's the better off for it.'
'You're confusing me,' I said, 'I'm more in
The dark now than I was before I asked.

How can goods that are shared make all those
With a share of them wealthier than if
They were possessed by just a few?'

'OK,' said Berrigan, 'think of it as being
Like that Welfare State that your country cherishes
So much. I know it's been fucked up by the

Tories, and by that wolf in sheep's clothing
Tony Blair, who we saw buried deep in the ice,
But the principle still stands: if everyone

Pays into the National Health Service, to take
Just the most obvious example, then the benefits
For each and every one of us are clear as daylight.

They say Covid-19's thrown this into perspective:
Here, the more we share, the more we own. On a less
Material level, think of love: the more people you open up to

In the spirit of love, the more love you get in return.
I know you'll say I'm just an old Beatnik
Hippy bodhisattva, but what I say is true.

Love breeds love. That's one of the things that Ginsberg
Can teach us, even if you don't need to get your
Cock out quite as much as he did to make the point.

And if this explanation still leaves you
Wondering, when you meet Marina, up above,
She'll be able to fill in any gaps.'

I was about to say 'I get it,' but
Seeing that we had now reached the next ledge,
My eyes left me tongue tied.

I don't know whether it was fatigue or
The lack of oxygen at that height or
The fact we hadn't eaten properly for

Some time or just the constant strain of one
New experience on top of another,
But it seemed to me that suddenly I

Was caught up in an ecstatic trance:
I saw a teacher being kicked and spat at
By a child who was totally out of control,

He threw books and chairs around the classroom,
Shouting 'Bitch!' and 'Cunt!' and 'I don't care!'
Yet when he had calmed down and sat in the

Sandpit, she spoke calmly to him, asking him
What was worrying him, what had disturbed him,
Inviting him to play with her in the sand.

The vision came and went in a moment,
And then another scene came into focus:
I saw a man stumble in a bar and touch

Another man on the hip to soften the impact,
Then I saw him bundled away by the police
And thrown into jail before he had a chance

To defend himself. People were calling
For his blood, when a man spoke out, it was
Sheikh Mohammed bin Rashid Al Maktoum,

Saying, 'What shall we do to those who wish
Us harm, if we condemn those who are harmless?'
And then I saw a jihadi, raging with hate,

Shooting at some off-duty policemen who were
Playing football in a field near Carcassonne,
And then I saw the same man, now

Shooting up a supermarket, and I saw a
Pale-faced gendarme, walking calmly into the store,
Offering himself up in exchange for a hostage.

When finally I flipped out of the trance,
And saw the ledge beneath my feet once more,
And, inches to my right, the sheer drop into the gulf,

I came back to reality with a start.
'What the fuck are you playing at?' said Berrigan.
'You're walking like a drunken man teetering

On a tightrope. Have you lost your senses?
Ever since we stepped on this ledge you've been
Unsteady on your legs, like someone half-asleep

Or flying high on benzedrine. Snap out of it!'
'Jesus,' I said, 'I think I drifted off
Into some kind of trance. I saw...' 'Don't tell

Me,' said Berrigan, 'even if you had a
Paper bag over your head I'm sufficiently
Tuned into your psyche to see what's going on in there.

The things you saw were shown you so that you
Could see the futility of anger –
This is the terrace where the angry are punished.

But if you fall off that ledge I'm the one
Who's going to lose his rag – I haven't brought you
All this way so you can throw yourself off a cliff.

Now, let's get moving.' We walked along
Through the evening light, looking ahead as far
As we could see, into the splendour of the setting sun.

Then gradually, a thick cloud of smoke came
Towards us, like a gathering storm, stinging our
Eyes, and taking away our sight.

There was no way for us to escape its fury.

## CANTO XVI

The darkness of Hell, or a night voided
Of all its stars, under a barren sky,
A sky overshadowed utterly by cloud,

Never drew such an impenetrable curtain
Across my sight, as that thick smoke which now
Enveloped us. Add to that the burning sensation

In my eyes in my throat and in my lungs,
An irritation so fierce and sudden that I could
Hardly breathe, and you will understand my panic

As we stepped into the smoke cloud, which was no
Ordinary cloud, I soon realised, but a cloud
Of tear gas, like the British Army used in the Troubles.

Berrigan rummaged in his backpack and handed
Me some ski goggles to protect my eyes,
And I used my sleeve to shield my mouth.

Holding tight to Berrigan's shoulder, as a
Blind man goes behind his guide, lest he lose his
Way or stumble into some obstacle in his path,

So I went through the acrid, poisonous air,
Listening to my master, who was warning me:
'Watch out! And cling on tight to me here.

Some of these dudes are dangerous men.'
I could hear voices, some raised, which were all
Heatedly discussing the Peace Process,

And all the sticking points in the Good Friday Agreement,
The same phrases, again and again, emerging
From the darkness, like a furious babble.

'Berrigan, these voices – are they shades I hear?'
I asked. And he replied: 'Yes, you've got it man,
They are the voices of former paramilitaries,

Catholics and Protestants alike, and men
From the SAS and the RUC, and they
Are untying the twisted knots of their anger.'

'Who the Hell are you, wee man, whose body cuts through
This tear gas? You speak of us as if you still belonged
To those who measure time by the ticking of a clock.'

Through burning ears I heard a voice somewhere
That uttered these words. Berrigan said: 'Give him
A straight answer, then ask how we get out of here.'

And so I spoke: 'Spirit, undoing the knot of
Anger, to secure the Peace Process, come
Closer, and I will tell you who I am.'

'I'll come with yeese as far as I'm allowed,' he said,
'They still keep a tight rein on the spirits locked here,
And if we cannot look on each other's faces,

We can at least hear each other's words.'
Then I went on: 'You guess right, friend, I'm from
The still-living world, still wrapped in the tissues I was

Born into in Belfast, though here I have lost all sense
Of time. I have travelled through the pains of the Infernal
Campus to arrive here, and now climb this mount.

But tell me who you were before you died,
And tell me too, if you can, is this the way to reach
The passage up? Your words shall be our guide.'

'I was an Ulsterman, McGuinness was my name,
I knew the worst of that country's doings, but turned to
The good for which men too seldom put down their guns,'

He said. Then, after a pause, he added: 'The path you're
On will take you to the stairs, and when you reach the top,
Be sure to put in a good word for me there.'

'You have my word on that,' I said, 'but there's
A question bugging me that I can no longer keep
To myself. Why is Ireland so fucked up?

You talk about putting down your guns, but why
Are there always some who turn to violence?
I'm thinking mostly of Ireland, but today it's something

We see across the globe, in Syria, in Ukraine
In Iraq and Afghanistan. Wherever you look.
What's the cause of this? Tell me, so that I can

Take your answer back home with me. Some say
That history is to blame, that tribal loyalties
Fuck us up from birth, or that some selfish gene

Pits us constantly against our neighbour.
Others say this is no excuse at all, and that
We should take responsibility ourselves.'

He gave a deep sigh, then coughed, uttering
'Jesus Christ!' Then he went on: 'The world is full of
Eejits, and I can see you have spent some time there,

But listen. I'm not the person to ask about
Genetics or biological determinism, but these things,
Together with the environment in which we are brought up,

While they have some effect on us, to be sure,
Can't be used as an excuse for what we do.
We all have the power to learn from our mistakes.

History isn't destiny. As Joyce said,
It's the nightmare from which we're trying to awake.
History, biology, tribal allegiance,

Environment, all these things affect our tendencies,
But they don't define us – and even if they did
That doesn't stop us telling right from wrong.

Whatever anyone says to the contrary
We still have free will, which, though it may be
Difficult to exercise at times, can still

Overcome apparently insurmountable
Obstacles – take Northern Ireland, the Peace Process
Has its critics, I know that as well as anybody,

But it still got bitter enemies talking,
And it has led to power sharing, which was
Unthinkable a decade ago. So,

If the world today looks fucked up to you,
The cause lies in yourselves and there only!
I know this for a fact, I've learned it the hard way.

I remember a friend of mine who used to be
In the IRA telling me about the time
He first saw the British Army in Belfast.

He witnessed the soldiers sealing off William Street,
And he was fascinated by all these men
With their helmets and rifles and backpacks.

He was excited by what he saw, and said to
Himself: "I am going to be a soldier someday."
And that's how he ended up in the IRA.

This was a personal decision, to be sure, but he could
Make it because the fools running the show thought
That armed struggle could lead to a united Ireland.

The leaders of the IRA had every reason
To grumble, but they lacked any historical
Perspective. What I'm saying is that the

Present state of the world is caused predominantly
By one thing and one thing alone: bad leadership.
And in the 70s there were bad leaders all round.

It's always been a bad idea to mix
Religion and politics, and it's a mistake
That Ireland has made time and again.

To give just one example, it was religion,
Not politics, which spelled the end for Parnell.
Mix the two, and society just breaks down along

Sectarian lines, as Belfast knows to its cost.
Under O'Neill's leadership there was still cause for hope,
He was committed to reform across communities,

But when things turned against him everything
Collapsed: the thugs and the paramilitaries
Roamed the streets unchecked, bringing terror

And torture and rough justice wherever they went.
There were a few good men who, if we'd only
Listened to them, could have put things on a different path.

I've mentioned O'Neill, he's one of them, but I'm
Thinking too of James Craig, and Basil Brooke,
Who once met Seán Lemass to discuss unification.'

'I've heard of O'Neill,' I said, 'but who are Craig and
Brooke?' 'You're having me on,' he said, 'you say you're a
Belfast man and you haven't heard of Jimmy Craig and

Basil Brooke? Craig was Ulster's first Prime Minister,
Later he was known as Lord Craigavon, I can't
Remember if Brooke went under another name –

He was his successor – God be with you! And now
I must turn back – I see a bright light penetrating
The smoke, this is as far as I can go.' And he turned,

Not giving me a chance to ask him more.

## CANTO XVII

Reader, if you have ever found yourself
Caught in a riot where the police throw tear gas
Canisters to disperse the angry crowd, trying to

Grope your way out of that cloud with stinging
Half-blinded eyes, like a sightless bat,
Remember how at last the thick toxic

Smoke starts to disperse, and how the sun's pale
Disc feebly begins to penetrate to street level,
Then you'll have some idea what it was like

When I caught sight of the sun again, now about to set.
Matching the steady footsteps of my guide,
I stumbled out of that cloud into the light

Whose rays were already dead on the low shore.
Whether it was the disorientation, or the burning
Effect of the tear gas I do not know,

But as I stood there coughing, doing my best
To breathe in the clean air and clear my lungs,
The powers of dream once more hijacked my mind,

Which now sunk so far into itself
That I lost all track of where we were
And what Berrigan was doing.

At first, as in a slide show,
I witnessed the furious anger of Procne
And Philomela, who were changed into songbirds.

Then poured into the bathtub of my soaring fantasy
The figure of a paranoid and angry
Paralympian, firing shot after shot

Through a closed bathroom door,
Until the woman screaming on the other side
Was silenced and lay dead on the floor.

Then, when this image of its own accord
Burst like a soap bubble when the shiny film
Around it pops, another vision arose

In my imagination – a tall red-faced man,
A poet whose face I half-recognised,
Stood with his hunched back towards me, beating

His wife, who shielded her face with outstretched hands,
And now I saw his friends turn their backs on him,
One by one, until he had no one to turn to.

When, suddenly, closed eyes are struck by light,
As sometimes happens when you leave the curtains
Open by mistake after a late night out,

Our sleep is disturbed, though it lingers on
A little before we fully waken.
Just so this vision began to slip away from me

When a light struck me across the face,
A light far brighter than anything I have seen on Earth.
Looking around confusedly to see where I was,

I saw the headlights of a St John's Ambulance,
But, as if staring at the burning sun
Whose brilliance overwhelms the sight and veils

Its very form, I could not see clearly for the glare.
A voice told me to lie down, and I heard
Berrigan's voice too from close by,

Explaining I had had a seizure on
Stepping out of the cloud of toxic CS gas.
I felt a damp cloth sponging my eyes clean

And another hand press an oxygen mask to my
Face – like those used for Covid-19 – and as I
Began to breathe more steadily and regain my bearings

I saw the face of an Alp Angel looking at me.
'He'll be alright in a few minutes,' she said to
Berrigan my guide, 'I've seen worse cases than this.'

When I had recovered enough strength to stand,
The Alp Angel showed us the stairs to the next terrace,
Then, letting our feet obey her call, we set off

To climb as far as we could in the fading light.
I was following Berrigan up the stairs, when he
Leant over and handed me my card, to which the

Alp Angel had added another stamp,
And as the two of us continued to climb I heard
The words 'Give peace a chance' uttered from behind us.

The sun's last rays, which would soon be followed by night,
Were already so low on the horizon
That stars began to poke through, here and there.

The climb was steep, and as I began to feel my strength
Fade, I kept repeating to myself 'You can do it Barry!'
As Barry Buxton used to say at Skoob,

When he was running out of steam after a long day.
I could feel all the force draining from my legs
When at last we reached the top of the stairs,

Where we found ourselves immobilised by exhaustion,
Whales beached on the shore. I waited for a
Moment, listening to hear if any sound issued

From this new round. Then, turning to Berrigan, I asked:
'What's the deal on this terrace? Though our feet have stopped,
Don't stop speaking to me.' And so, at length, he said:

'OK, to put it in a nutshell, everyone
Here is a bit like Tony Tackling, who we met below –
Here the once-sluggish cyclist pedals for all he's worth,

And then some. But if you want a better outline of
The whole kit and caboodle, Zones 1-7,
Then prick up your ears, so we can profit from this pause.

Those of a religious persuasion
Would probably explain the logic of
The mount by talking about "love" and "God",

But for someone with a more secular
Frame of mind like yours, it's probably best
Explained by thinking of it in terms of desire.

Every child is born in desire,' he went on,
'We know this from experience as well
As from psychoanalysis. The child's first

Love object is its mother – that's the start
Of the Oedipal phase – but later on it
Chooses other objects, like dogs

Or ponies, or dolls, or chocolate.
As it grows up it will alter these objects,
You could say it's because desire always wants more,

So instead of a doll, it might fall in love
With a real person, a kind of mother substitute,
Right? This is where things can start to go wrong.

What if the person falls in love with a biker?
Or a cocaine addict? What if they now fall in love
With chocolate again and start binging on it?

You see where I'm going with this? Desire can
Move mountains, but it can also fuck up badly.
If it runs along the right tracks then everything's cool,

But that's not something you can take for granted.
So, if you follow me, love, or desire, whatever
You call it, is not only a source of good,

But a lot of bad shit too – if you love guns
And the smell of blood, at best you'll end up
Shooting pheasants to get your kicks,

At worst you'll become a dictator, fuelled
By hatred – that's why people say that
Love and hate are two sides of the same coin.

In masochism too love turns to hatred
And is directed against the self, but more
Often hate is directed against others.

So, this warped desire becomes directed
Against other people, like your neighbours,
Or your colleagues, or foreigners, as in Brexit.

This can happen in many ways, but there are
Three which are common and which underpin
The organisation of the mountain.

Firstly, there are the egos, the proud, people
Who think the sun shines out of their arses,
And people like this always like to see their peers

In difficulty, for it bolsters their own sense of success:
That's why the tabloids do so well by filling their
Pages with stories of footballers in disgrace.

Secondly, and not all that different at the end of
The day, there are the jealous types, those who hate to see
Others climb the social ladder, who like to kick people

When they're down. There are plenty of Conservative MPs
With this mindset, who delight in rationalising
The benefits of those who have nothing.

Finally, there are those who, when they perceive they have
Been wronged or threatened, fly into a rage, and in their
Passion for revenge seek to harm others, I'm sure you can

Think of examples yourself – Hamlet's one of the prototypes.
These three perversions of desire are punished in
The three circles we've travelled through below.

This circle, as I say, punishes the slackers,
While the three that follow punish desire
That is at once misdirected and excessive,

As you'll be able to see for yourself later.'

## CANTO XVIII

When he had finished talking, Berrigan
Lit a Chesterfield, blowing smoke rings into
The night air, his back turned towards me.

And I, already itching to ask him more questions,
Kept silent, thinking he's probably fed up
To the back teeth with this endless Q&A.

But Berrigan, that true father, read my mind,
Which was too timid to express itself.
'What's bugging you?' he said. 'Spit it out!'

'What you were saying just now,' I said, 'I think
I get the gist of it, but it's a lot to take in
At once. Your discourse has enlightened me,

But can you tell me some more about
This thing you call "love" or "desire", which is, you say,
The source of every virtue and every vice?'

'Shine on me, dude,' he said, 'the flashing lights
Of your intellect, and I'll tell you what I can
About the workings of love. Love is blind,

Every poet knows that, that's why Cupid
Is always depicted with a blindfold, right?
*A Midsummer Night's Dream* is one of the

Great expressions of this in literature.
The mind, which is created ready to love,
Is set off by anything that is pleasing,

As soon as pleasure wakes it up for action.
So Lysander, awaking, falls in love with Helena.
Your apprehension carries the impression

From a real object, and displays it inside you,
As on a screen, and the mind turns towards it.
That's love, or desire, whatever you choose to call it.

From a psychoanalytic point of view, its the
Unconscious which is in control here, and like Cupid
The unconscious is blind, or rather we are blind to its

Workings. For Freud, the infant is polymorphous
Perverse, kind of attracted to everything; later,
Desire will focus on a particular love object,

Like the mother's breast, or a page 3 girl.
In Narcissism, say, the love object is the self,
The ego – which for Lacan is a fictional construct –

He explains this in "The Mirror Phase", though
There isn't time to go into that here.
Freud puts it more clearly, perhaps, when he divides

Childhood sexuality into successive phases:
The oral, the anal, and the phallic.
But what he calls normal development

Can go pear-shaped at any point: get stuck
In the anal phase and you might fall in
Love with your own excrement. Perhaps Yeats

Knew more than he was letting on when he wrote:
"Love has pitched his mansion in the place of excrement."
I'm beginning to ramble, but to put it in a

Nutshell, you can easily see that while love
May always feel like a good thing, those luvvies
Who claim it is always a force for the good

Are wildly mistaken. Love can take a wrong turn, and it
Can suck you into dark places – just think of Charles Manson
Or the moors murderers, and you'll see what I'm getting at.'

'I think I've got the picture,' I said, 'but some
Of what you say still puzzles me. If love
Comes from a source outside of us, as in

The mirror reflection discussed by Lacan –
For I taught that essay once in Exmouth,
Chewing over its ins and outs with Liz Farr –

The "hommelette", to use another of Lacan's terms,
Having no say in the matter, how can you praise
Or blame it for its love of good or bad?'

And Berrigan to me: 'I can only explain to you
What I understand – for the rest you'll have to
Wait for Marina, she has a better grasp of these things.

Every human form, being distinct from inert
Matter, yet somehow conjoined with it,
Contains, as I said, its unconscious drives,

Invisible except as they are made manifest
In Freudian slips, and through the dreamwork,
Where careful analysis can detect their workings.

So, to put it bluntly, hominids cannot know
Where their primary impulses come from – or their bent
For those primary objects of desire.

Lacanian theory makes this explicit, by making
The theory itself so complex, with the *objet*
*Petit "a"* for example, that our minds cannnot grasp it.

These drives are part of you, just like the zeal
Of bees for making honey, and this primal will, or
Libido, is neither to be praised nor blamed.

But you still have your common sense, man,
And what Freud calls the superego,
Which can police the thresholds of desire.

These are the principles on which are based
The judgement of your merit – according as it
Separates the good love from the bad.

Those pioneers who with their reason probed the depths
Of the mind, perceived these primal drives, innate in us all,
Thus bequeathing psychoanalysis to the world.

And even if we say that every love that burns
In you arises through sheer necessity,
You still have the power to restrain such love.

This ability Marina would call the
Freedom to choose, the freedom of the will – remember
That if she happens to mention it to you.'

It was almost midnight. The late-risen moon,
Which rested like a newborn sickle in the sky,
Now made the stars seem fewer in number.

That goofy shade, who had made Providence
Renowned above all towns on Rhode Island, was now
Free from the burden I had laid on him,

And I, who had been privileged to reap
Such clear, straight answers to my questions,
Let my thoughts wander sleepily;

Yet this lazy mood was shortlived,
For suddenly we heard a rush of wheels
Coming around the mount behind our backs,

And as the Cam and Cherwell, on graduation day,
Will see along their brightly-lit banks the
Rush and rage of drunken students on bicycles,

Just such a frenzied crowd I thought I saw
When that dense rush of cycles curved round the bank,
Spurred in their race by goodwill and punishing targets.

And then it was upon us – that whole
Enormous peloton on the move.
Two out in front were shouting as they went:

‘Eric Gilbert wrote his doctorate in three months!’ cried one,
The other: ‘Liza Granville to fund her PhD
Had to work nights in a sandwich factory!’

‘Faster! Faster! We haven’t a moment to lose,
For time is funding,’ cried others from behind,
‘We need to hit our deadlines and complete in three years!’

‘Hey! You students, whose eager pedalling atones,
I’m guessing, for past delay and negligence,
In dawdling over a thesis for too long –

This man, I swear it, is alive, and he
Would like to climb to the top when day returns,
Can you show us the way to reach the cleft?’

These were Berrigan’s words. One of the shades
Shouted out as he pedalled by: ‘Follow the crowd,
That way you’ll find the passage by yourself!

We can’t stop, the desire to race keeps
Pushing us on – so don’t take it to heart
If our penance seems discourteous.

I was an Essex PhD if you want to know
When Albert Sloman was VC –
Those he suspended over the Porton Down protest

Still speak of him with bitterness. There’s another
VC now living in retirement who will soon
Have cause to rue the power *he* wielded once

Over that campus: instead of a true pastor
He put as head a military man deformed
In mind who runs the place like a boot…'

If he said more, I could not hear the words,
The pair of us were left so far behind,
But I was glad to hear as much as I did.

Then Berrigan, who was still standing at my side,
Said: 'Turn around, take a look at these postgrads here,
Both pedalling madly to atone their sloth.'

Behind the rest these two were calling: 'All of those
For whom the British Academy provided funding
Without question were dead before their citation

Rates hit double figures; and those who found the task
Too difficult ditching their PhDs after ten years
Toil gave themselves up to an inglorious life.'

Then, when those spirits had raced so far ahead
That they were completely out of sight,
Another thought took shape in my mind,

Creating others besides, by association,
So that from thought to thought my mind began
To wander as in sleep, before I closed my eyes,

Letting my thinking dissolve into dream.

## CANTO XIX

It was the hour when the central heating comes on
To take away the chill of the night air,
And commuters reluctantly rise from their beds –

When astrologers see Fortuna Major
Rise on the sunshine coast, just before dawn,
Across from beach huts soon to be bathed in light.

In my dreams I saw a half-crazed woman
With too much rouge on her cheek, and a black eye,
Struggling to walk her heels were so high,

Her hands were fidgeting, all her colour was washed out.
At first I just stood there staring at her, immobile,
Yet as the sun revives a body chilled by the cold night,

Just so my eyes as they gazed upon her
Worked to straighten her gait and to sweeten
Her features and smooth out all her deformities,

Gradually suffusing her fuck-off face
Until it was just as desire itself would paint it.
And now her tongue too seemed loosened by my gaze

And she began to sing – and the sweetness of her song,
Like Joanna Newsom, captivated all my senses.
'I am,' she sang, 'the sweet siren,

My song beguiles the sailors on the sea,
My song beguiles the midnight surfer,
Enticing them to come to me!'

Before her painted lips had closed, a fearsome woman –
She was the spitting image of Germaine Greer –
Loomed up suddenly at my side, and started to berate my guide:

'Ted Berrigan,' she spat, 'who the Hell is this
You're introducing to your friend when you should be
Setting him an example, is this your idea of a joke?

Did you learn nothing from that party you went to in Chicago
Where all the girls wore those humiliating no front dresses
Parading around with their tits hanging out for inspection?

Do you think that's the future? Wake up, Ted!'
Berrigan now stumbled towards the singer, shamefaced, galvanised
Into action – he ripped out the porn star's microphone,

Then tore down a screen which served for her backdrop,
On which were projected waves lapping the shore of some
Generic tropical island, to reveal behind it,

Crouched in clouds of smoke over a wad of money and a
Mountain of cocaine, a bunch of pimps and porn barons
And minders and fat business tycoons and hangers-on.

The stink of their cigars woke me up with a start,
Then I turned to see Berrigan gesticulating close at my side.
'For Christ's sake, man, get moving you jackoff,

I've called you at least ten times! Shift your butt,
And let's find the opening that you're looking for!'
I stood up slowly, feeling slightly dazed –

Daylight had now spread out across all the
Terraces of the Essex Alp – then we
Moved on, the new sun warm on our backs.

Following close in Berrigan's footsteps,
Head bent low, and brooding on my troubled thoughts
(I must have looked like the half arch of an

Unfinished
            Andy Goldsworthy sculpture)
I suddenly heard a voice from up ahead say:

'Over here, travellers, this way, this is the way through!'
Spoken in so kind and gentle a manner
As one rarely hears in this world of ours.

We saw then, not far ahead, the form of
One of the Alp's Angels, arms outstretched, like wings,
Inviting us to make our way upwards

Between two walls of hard blue sandstone.
As we made our way up the narrow path
He chatted to us as we went, and when

He heard I was from Ireland he began to reminisce
About walking in the Morne Mountains from where he'd
Once hiked all the way to the Giant's Causeway.

We talked about climbing Slieve Donard,
And Tollymore Forest Park. When we reached
The guide's cabin, he added another stamp to my card,

Then we left him at his post, moving on.
We'd only advanced a few paces when
Berrigan turned to me and said: 'What's eating you son?

Why are you staring so at the ground?'
'It's nothing, I'm feeling a bit shagged out, that's all,
And I guess that dream I had is still bugging me.'

'You saw,' he said, 'into the world of corruption
Where sex is exploited as a commodity
By rich businessmen, whose only goal is

The accumulation of wealth, and the power that
Comes with it, regardless of the cost. These are
The sort of souls we'll meet grieving above.

But you saw too how to escape that trap,
So don't let it bug you. Now, let's move on,
There's a way to go, and the sky's our goal.'

Just as the peregrine falcon, who has been gazing at
Its feet, turns suddenly at the call, spreading
Its wings, ready to soar towards the bait,

Such was I – I strained to reach the end of the
Narrow cleft in the rock, to enter on another
Circling ledge, little knowing what lay ahead.

When I was out in the open again, on the fifth terrace,
I saw people lying face down on the ground who wept,
Their feet and hands bound tightly with gaffer tape.

'*Another One Bites the Dust!*' I heard ring out,
Accompanied by a heavy bass riff
That almost made the words inaudible.

'Hey there dustbiters, I dig your theme tune,
And I hope it makes your suffering easier to bear –
But can you tell us the way to reach the stairs?'

'If you have been exempt from lying flat,
And wish to find the quickest way ahead,
Just keep your right hand to the outer edge.'

So did the poet ask, and so the answer came,
From somewhere close in front of us – so close, indeed,
I could make out the back of the head that spoke.

I fixed my eyes upon my master's,
And there I saw the playful gleam of his consent
To the desire which my look expressed. And then,

Once free to do as I wished,
I walked ahead and stood over that soul
Whose voice had caught my attention earlier.

'Spirit,' I said, 'you whose tears ripen
That without which no one returns to good,
I beg you, interrupt your task

A moment, tell me who you were and why
You all lie flat like that. Is there some way that I
Can help you in the world I left alive?'

‘Why Heaven has set our backsides towards itself,’
The spirit said, ‘you soon will hear, but first
Know that I was the successor of McNamara.

Near the border of Cork and Kerry, you’ll find the
Barony of Upper Connello, and from its
Name comes the title of my family, Connell.

All too soon I learned how the Primate’s garments
Weigh on he who wishes to keep the church’s name out
Of the mud – compared to that, all else is featherweight,

Even the punishment we suffer here,
And the mountain knows no harsher penalty.
To come back to your question, putting it bluntly,

We lie like this to cure the greed
We displayed on Earth. Just as our eyes,
Attached to worldly goods, would never leave

The Earth to look above, so here they are forced
To the ground, our feet and hands tightly bound,
As avarice bound all our love of good.

I wasn’t avaricious in the common sense,
But when the church was rocked by child abuse
Scandals and accused of secretly paying

Compensation to victims to shut them up,
I was parsimonious with the truth.
I learned the whole story too late, and only

When I had been Archbishop for some years
Did the full extent of the abuse become clear:
It was a shocking and damning tale from start to finish.'

As it dawned on me who was speaking, I got
Down on my knees, and I was about to speak
Myself, when the Primate of all Ireland

Cut me off, asking: 'Why are you kneeling at my side?'
And I replied: 'You are the Primate of Ireland, your…'
'Up on your feet, now, young man, I'll be having

None of that here. You should not kneel before
Such as I, we are all equals here –
I am no longer wedded to my archdiocese.

Do not stay any longer. Leave me now.
Your presence at my side halts the flow of tears
That ripens what you spoke about before.

I have grandnieces on Earth, good girls, I pray their
Names stay out of the press and that they never get caught
Up in the scandals that have so engulfed my later years –

They are all I have left in the world.'

## CANTO XX

I'd have happily gone on talking for a while longer,
But he'd had enough of my questions, so I
Left him where he lay, and put away my notebook,

The page unfilled. Berrigan negotiated
The track ahead, sticking close to the cliff,
Wherever there was space to tread,

For on the other side those sprawling shades,
Who distill in tears the greed for gain that gobbles up
The planet, were too close to the drop for comfort.

'Fuck you capitalism, you couldn't give a shit
About anything except your profit margins!
Take a good look at your kind, crawling like worms

On the edge of this mountain, and tell
Me if any six-figure bonus can help them now?
Your never-sated appetite has claimed more victims

Than any plague or famine or natural disaster.
When will the day come when we ditch you for
Good, like toxic waste in a bottomless landfill?'

We went on with slow and cautious steps,
My mind fixed on those shades that I heard
Grieving and sobbing so piteously.

Then I happened to catch a voice from
Somewhere up ahead wailing 'Holy Mary!'
Like a woman off *Call The Midwife* crying out in labour.

And then right after: 'How poor you were is
Plain from the lousy accommodation you
Shared when you dropped your sacred load.'

And then I heard: 'Ah, good Bullimore, you
Preferred to stay true to yourself on a miserable wage,
Rather than ingratiate yourself with the rich.'

I was so intrigued by what I heard that
I quickened my pace to find the spot I
Thought the words were coming from, eager to

See the shade who had just spoken;
He went on, speaking of that generous
Philanthropist, Sylvia La Terre, who

Spent her fortune helping former sex workers
Find safe houses and independence.
'Hello,' I said, 'I couldn't help hearing your voice,

Tell me who you were, and tell me why you
Alone lie here praising generous hearts.
If you can give me an answer, then do,

And if I live to tell my tale back on Earth,
Before my days are done I promise to put
In a good word for you among the living.'

'I will answer you,' he said solemnly,
'Not out of hope for any help from your world, but
Because of the balls you show in coming here at all.

I was the root of that malignant tree
Which overshadowed the oil industry
In the 1970s, from which no good fruit is plucked.

Even the princes of Saudi Arabia
Had nothing on me – so great was my wealth
I had them eating out of my hand.

I was known as Jean Paul Getty in the world: from
Me sprang those John Pauls the second and the third
By whom our business has recently been rocked.

I was the son of an attorney in
The insurance industry, a shrewd man,
From whom I learned thrift and the value of oil.

At twenty-one I was given $10,000 to invest
In oil fields in Oklahoma. We struck oil within
A year and by the next August I was a millionaire.

I found the dynasty's reins clutched in my hands,
And its whole government, and so much power
That once I tasted it I cried out for more.

I had wished to place the business in the hands of
My son George, but he was a disappointment to me.
The pressure must have been too much for him,

So he turned to drugs, then took his own life
In the most horrible manner, stabbing
Himself to death with a barbecue fork.

Worse was to come. My grandson made a fool
Of us all with a photoset in *Playgirl*,
And ran up a huge debt in Italy over cocaine.

Worse was to come. In a botched attempt to
Pay off his debts he staged a kidnapping.
We knew right off there was something funny

About it all, and ignored the ransom requests.
I still don't know how it all came about,
But at one point what had all started off as

A bad joke turned bitter. In the sort of twist
Of fate that could only happen in Italy,
A group of upstart Calabrian Mafiosi

Kidnapped him for real. The ransom was absurd,
$17,000,000, and I refused to pay –
I didn't want to put the whole family in jeopardy.

Eventually we negotiated them down,
At no inconsiderable risk to myself, I could add.
I organised a loan, on generous terms,

For the boy's father, but he refused to sign.
He was another disappointment, another one
Who wasted his life dabbling in drugs.

Worse was to come. The boy's ear turned up in the post.
It was the last straw, so I decided to pay
Myself, going halves with the boy's father.

And that was that. He was returned to his
Family, minus the ear. I cut off all ties with the boy
After that and never spoke to him again.

Oh, avarice, what worse lies in wait for our family,
Now that we have become so close to you
We don't even care for our own flesh and blood?

To make the past and future look less dire,
I built the Getty Villa and the
Getty Centre, outside Los Angeles, by the sea,

To make a permanent home for my art collection,
And to carry out research into art history.
Though the vinegar and gall didn't stop here –

Critics called my Getty Villa vulgar
And compared it to Disneyland,
Then after this my wives drifted off,

One by one. I guess they could see my true
Love was oil – you either make a successful business
Or a successful marriage, you can't have both.

When you saw me back there, calling out to
Mary, that one true bride – that's what we
All do here while the daylight still lasts,

But when night falls we turn to greed for our theme.
In darkness, we call up Pygmalion, who murdered his
Sister Dido's husband, to stuff his pockets with gold.

We tell how Midas suffered when his miser's prayer
Was answered, how he starved as his food turned
To gold, how he ended in ludicrous despair.

Then we remember Achan, who stole the spoils
Of Jericho, and was stoned to death for his sacrilege.
There's a striking painting of the scene in the Jewish

Museum in New York, by Joseph Tissot,
You should check it out if you ever go there,
And there's Blake's version too, "The Blasphemer".

Then we accuse Sapphira and her husband,
We praise the hooves that kicked Heliodorus,
Then the Essex Alp resounds to the infamous

Polymnestor, who murdered the boy Polydorus,
As Virgil tells. Last of all we cry: "Crassus,
Tell us, for you know, what flavour does gold have?"

At times one of us calls out loud, while another
Whispers softly, as the urge takes us. We are
Like Quakers here, and only speak when moved

To do so. So when I called out in praise
Of those generous spirits, I was not alone as
You thought, it was just that others held their peace.'

We had already left that shade behind,
And leaning on our sticks struggled as best we could
To make progress across that difficult terrain,

When suddenly, as though jelly-moulds were
Crashing down from the high walls of Hell's
Kitchen, I felt the mountain quake and tremble,

At which point an icy coldness clutched me,
As it clutches one that goes to his death.
The Millennium Bridge never shook so violently

Before the engineers at Arup shored it up
With inertial and fluid-viscous dampers.
Then all around we heard calamitous shouts,

So loud that Berrigan, my guide, drew close
To me, and held me tightly in his arms: 'Just keep
Cool,' he said, 'I'm not going to let you down now.'

'Let's party!' they all shouted together,
And 'Dude!' as I could hear from those nearest,
Whose shouts were clear enough to make out.

We stopped and waited for the commotion to pass,
All the while the ground trembling beneath our feet,
Until the quake ceased and the cries died down.

Then we continued on our solitary road
Still gazing at the shades prostrated on the ground,
Who once more began their Quaker's round.

Never before or since, unless my memory
Is playing up, had my blind ignorance
Stirred up in me such a desire to know

What was going on. Yet because we were in
A hurry, I didn't dare ask Berrigan,
Nor could I figure it out for myself,

So I went on, timid and lost in thought.

## CANTO XXI

'All men by nature desire to know,' says
Aristotle in his *Metaphysics*,
And terrified by the quake that had just

Shaken the mountain *I* was anxious to know
What its cause might be, worried that we were
In danger, and what we should do in an emergency.

Fear drove me to hurry along
The cluttered path, dodging the helpless
Bodies that lay prostrate in their pain,

Like the injured piled in a tube station
After some catastrophe on the line.
Then suddenly – just as you will read in the Gospel

According to Luke that Christ, new-risen from the
Hollow tomb, appeared to the two men on the
Emmaus road – a shade appeared beside us!

He had come up from behind us as we
Were trying not to step on the prostrate forms,
And we were unaware of him till he spoke.

'Greetings, Earthlings!' he said. 'Peace be with you.'
At once, we quickly turned to face him, and Berrigan
Answered him, grinning, with the Vulcan sign for peace.

'May the law that sentenced me to eternal
Banishment,' said Berrigan, 'grant you the keys
Of the mountain, and speed you to the top!'

'No kidding,' he said, obviously taken aback,
'Are you guys from Hell? So how have you managed to climb
Up this far without running into security?'

And then Berrigan, my guide, said: 'If you
Check out all the stamps that the Alp Angels have put
On my friend's card you'll see that he has the right to climb.

But this dude is still among the living,
Therefore he could not make the ascent himself,
And so I was called up from the wide throat of Hell

To serve him as guide, and guide him I shall,
As far as my schooling can take him.
But tell me, man, have you any idea

Why the mountain shook like that just now,
And why all of the souls from here down to its
Marshy base cried out together as they did?'

My guide's question, as so often before,
Threaded the needle's eye of my desire, and I
Listened carefully to what the shade said, all ears.

'The climate here is artificially regulated,
Just as the mountain itself is artificial.
Essex is a dry county, but here there's

No rain at all, nor is there any hail,
Sleet, or snow – which is a shame, for sure, as
It would be great for sledging. Likewise, you won't

Find any dew or any frost forming
At any point above the gateway down below.
With rare exceptions, there are no clouds,

Misty or dense, there's nothing for Constable here,
And there's no lightning, either, which you might
Expect on such an exposed mountain.

Quakes may occur below, slight or severe,
For we are not that far from the Wivenhoe fault,
But such tremors have never reached this high –

They are absorbed by the Flexible Rock Substitute
From which the mountain is constructed – which
Neutralises any tremor like a shock absorber.

Up here the mountain trembles when some soul
Feels itself ready to stand up and climb –
And when that happens the shout follows.

I've been lying here for longer than I
Care to remember, and felt only now the will
To raise myself up and climb to a higher sill.

You always know the moment when it arrives,
It's like a rush of super-cool karma, and it's
Well worth the wait – I'd recommend it to anyone.

That's why you felt the quake and why you heard
The shouts – it's nothing to worry about, up here it
Happens all the time, and we celebrate it with a yell.'

This was the shade's explanation, and as he
Finished I felt myself overcome with joy,
For the more he spoke the more I felt sure

That this was the soul of a poet I knew
From down below – his hair was a little greyer,
And he was taller than I remembered him,

But without a doubt this was the body
Of Tim Atkins. From the way he looked at us
I could tell he hadn't recognised me.

I hadn't changed *that* much, I thought, my hair,
Certainly, was tousled by the arduous climb,
I hadn't put on any hair gel for days,

And I was starting to grow a beard, and then
I remembered his myopia, which was one thing even
This mountain wouldn't cure. Stepping up to him –

There was no Covid here, remember – I gave him a
Big hug: 'Hey, Tim, it's me! The poet you gave his first
Reading to, whose Dante you first published in *Onedit!*'

'Man,' he said, 'I never thought I'd meet you here!
How are things?' I was about to start, when Berrigan
My guide, butted in. 'I don't think I've had

The pleasure,' he said, 'but please, tell me in
Your own words who you once were, and why
You have been on this terrace for so long.'

'During the age of Ashbery, who, with
The undying support of Michael Schmidt
On this side of the Atlantic, through thick

And thin, mostly thin, came to define an era,
I bore the same title on my passport, that of poet,
That guarantees anonymity and little reward.

From the Malvern hills, London called me,
And judged me worthy to read at X-ing the Line,
And I taught, one summer, at the Jack Kerouac

School of Disembodied Poetics. My name
Is Atkins, Tim Atkins, and you'll hear people
Talk about me wherever they talk about jazz and poetry.

I translated Horace, then the complete Petrarch,
Before turning to novels for my verse,
When everyone else started versioning.

The spark that kindled my poetic ardour
Came from the sacred flame that set a whole
Generation on fire: I mean the New York School.

That was the mother of my poetry,
The nurse that gave me her teat, without Ashbery,
Padgett, and above all Ted Berrigan,

My verses would not be worth a fuck.
When I worked at UEL I used to envy
Those who valued the poetry of J.H. Prynne,

For they were able to hang out with their hero
In Cambridge, undisturbed by women,
While I had no such luck – I'd hoped, on

Coming here, to meet a few poets I valued,
But until now I haven't met a soul,
Just earnest business types and ex-priests,

Though it's a multi-faith mountain, I'm told.
If only I could have been alive when Berrigan lived,
I'd spend an extra year on this terrace.'

At these words Berrigan turned to me. His look
Told me in silence: 'Shut the fuck up!' But the power
Of the human will is often useless:

Laughter and tears follow so close on the heels
Of the emotions that set them off, that the older
The man, the less they will obey his will.

I smiled then wiped my expression blank quicker
Than a blink, but he stopped speaking; staring straight at
Me, right up close, Atkins missed nothing.

'I'm sure you didn't come here to mock the
Inmates,' he said sharply. 'Now, tell me the
Reason for your smile a moment ago,

That smile that went as quickly as it came.'
Now I was caught between two opposing sides,
One says be quiet, one says speak up.

And so I stood, rooted to the spot, saying nothing.
My guide took control of the situation: 'Spill the
Fucking beans, man,' he said, 'and answer the question.'

'You find my smiling here strange,' I said to the
Moody Atkins, 'but there is something
I must tell you that is stranger still.

This shade here who guides me up the mount
Is none other than the poet Ted Berrigan.
Step a little closer and see for yourself.

Straight up, the only reason I smiled, is
That you chose to mention Berrigan right now:
Your own words are to blame.'

Already, he was bending down to embrace
My guide's feet, but Berrigan said: 'Stop right
There, brother! You are a mere shade, and it

Is another shade you see before you.'
And Atkins, rising, said, 'Man, now you
Understand how my love for you burns deep,

When I deal with shadows as with solid things.'

## CANTO XXII

We'd already left the Alp Angel behind us,
The guide who had shown us to the sixth terrace –
He'd added a stamp to my card,

Then told us to look out for those who thirst
After the good, stressing the *thirst*, and all this he
Did so swiftly there'd barely been time to thank him –

When I, feeling lighter than at the other openings,
Went on with a surer tread, so that without effort now
I was keeping track with the swift spirits as they climbed.

Now, Berrigan was already speaking: 'Love,
Kindled by beauty, always kindles more love,
If the flame burns bright,

And so, ever since the day that Tom Raworth
Came down to Hell's Limbo to join us,
Telling me of your great regard for my writing,

I have felt nothing but good will towards you, more than
I've felt for any poet I hadn't met, and so
This tedious climb will now seem much shorter.

But tell me – let's cut the formalities,
Speak to me as you might to an old friend,
And forgive me if I speak too boldly –

How on Earth could your heart find room for *greed*,
For your poetry is full only of wit
                                        and good sense?'

At these words Atkins let a brief smile play
Over his lips, and fade. Then he replied:
'I'm touched by everything you say.

Buddhism has taught me that appearances
Will often cause people to jump to strange
Conclusions, when the truth lies elsewhere.

By your question I'm guessing that you think
That on Earth I was marked by that greed which
Instills itself in the heart of every consumer,

Leaving them constantly lusting for greater material wealth.
As you say in "Rusty Nails": "We are drawn to shit because
We are imperfect in our uses of the good."

Well, it's not surprising, given where you found me,
But in truth, if I had a fault it was
Not giving a shit about money.

If anything, I was a good old-fashioned spendthrift,
Especially when it came to books and CDs and vinyl.
Know then, I ended up on this terrace

Among these souls who weep for avarice
Because my fault was the opposite of theirs.
It's one of the strange laws of the mountain

And you don't need to have to read Derrida
To understand it – when any inclination is the rebuttal
Of its opposite, the two of them wither together here.'

'Now, when you sang about the bitter love
Of Petrarch, or versioned Horace's odes,'
The bard of *Many Happy Returns* said to him,

'I see no trace of that fruit which you so
Openly profess now – so tell me, what
Heavenly sun or what Earthly beam lit up your

Course so that you could set sail behind the Buddha?'
Atkins said: 'It was through your work, and more
Generally that of the New York School,

That I first started writing poetry –
My *Twenty-five Sonnets* comes straight out of that drawer.
It was the same school that showed me the path to Buddhism.

You can hardly deny that your own work,
For all its apparent personalism,
Ultimately rests on an aesthetic of impersonality,

Where the self is dissolved in the vertigo
Of borrowed and recycled texts which are
Forever reborn in different forms.

It's more about the method than anything else,
And the same is true of my own poetry –
My favourite sequence in *Petrarch* is the

Series of poems where words are progressively
Replaced by their definitions – this was
Liberating for me as I had no part in it as ego.

But tell me, how come you're familiar with
My work – most of it, no, *all* of it, appeared
After you death in 1983 was it?'

To which Berrigan replied: 'We're not barred
Reading material in Limbo – there's no "book ban"
which gives it the edge over the British penal system –

In fact we have quite a good library down there,
And if a book's not in stock there's an
Excellent inter-library loan service.

Still, I find it strange that you took
Religious inspiration from *my* work.'
'You're forgetting how attuned you were to the zeitgeist,'

Said Atkins. 'You were the lonely traveller in the dark
Who held his torch out behind him, casting a beam of light,
Not for his own benefit, but to teach others;

For even if you avoided adherence
To any faith yourself beyond your pills,
Preferring like Keats to live in doubt and

Uncertainty, your words pointed the way
To your disciples, you even said it straight out,
This one even you can't deny, in your

"Three Sonnets and a Coda for Tom Clark":
"Being a new day my heart
Is confirmed in its pure Buddhahood."'

Realising that here was a poet
Who had read Berrigan's work more closely
Than he had himself, for once Berrigan shut up.

Then, after a pause, Atkins resumed: 'Now,
Please tell me, you who removed the veil
That once hid from me the good I sing,

Tell me, while there is still some way to climb,
Where is our ancient Horace, do you know?
And Petrarch, and Celan, and Akhmatova?

Have they been damned? If so, where are they lodged?'
'They all, along with Dorn and me
And others,' said my guide, 'are with that American

The muses suckled more that all the rest,
In the First Zone of the Infernal Campus.
We often fantasise about the mountain

Slope where our nine muses hang out.
Hawkins walks with us, whose work you know,
Lopez and Barnett are there too, as well as

Corcoran, who wrote *Helen Mania*, and
Others who have taken inspiration from Greece.
With us are many of your New York School too:

O'Hara, Ron Padgett, Clark Coolidge,
Bernadette Mayer, sad as she has ever been,
And he who showed Brainard to the French.

Of the others you might know, too many to name,
There's Marjorie Perloff, and her daughter Nancy,
And Antonia Byatt, with her sister too.'

The poets now were at the top of the stairs,
And both of them stood in silence on the ledge,
Eager once more to gaze out at everything.

Then Berrigan said: 'I think we ought to shift,
Keeping our right shoulders to the outside edge,
The way we always have done round this Essex Alp.'

So, habit was our guide now, and we went on
Our way with much less hesitation than before,
Since Atkins gave us the go-ahead.

Berrigan and Atkins strode ahead and I followed
Close behind, paying close attention to their words,
As they discussed the secrets of their art.

Atkins talked about the different methods
Of translation he employed, citing Oulipo
And the work of Douglas Barbour and Stephen Scobie,

Berrigan, for his part, talked about how much
He had learnt from New York collage artists,
How this had given him the courage to

Cut up and mix different texts to the point where
He had no idea where his own lines came from.
At which point Atkins began to talk about

The time some friends had presented him with some lines
Of verse and quizzed him about their authorship. The lines,
It turned out, were his own, but he hadn't recognised them.

'A good line of poetry,' he said, 'is never
Personal, if it works, it just takes its place in the
Indistinguishable mass of poetry in the world.'

Then, right in the middle of the path, a tree appeared,
Laden with fruit whose sticky perfume filled the air,
And suddenly that poetry talk was cut short.

Just as a fir tree tapers towards the top, so
This one tapered down, like an inverted Christmas tree,
To stop the souls from climbing, I guess.

On that side where our way was bounded poured
Clear water from an outlet in the rock,
Sprinkling the topmost branches in a cascade.

As the two poets drew close, there came a mechanical voice
That barked at us from within the tree:
'*This fruit and this water are out of bounds!*'

Then the voice ground to a halt as if the mechanism
Had failed, before starting up again – *bdzzzzzzzzrrrkk!* –
And repeating what it had said already.

'I don't think this exhibit is working
As it should be,' said Berrigan, 'let's see if the
Guidebook offers any illumination.'

He leafed through the pages, adjusting his
Spectacles, then read out the following
Passage: 'After a gentle stroll along

The sixth terrace, the visitor will encounter
The unmistakable "Fountain Tree", unique
To the British Isles. It is not upside down, as it

Appears at first sight, but has a vertical branch
Growth pattern which increases in girth as the tree
Increases in height. The first visitors to the

Terrace would have been greeted by recorded voices
Extolling the virtues of abstinence, exemplified
By the stories of Mary, Daniel, and John the Baptist,

Who subsisted on a diet of locusts and honey.
This feature has been removed until further notice.
The management accepts no responsibility

For those who adopt these figures as role models.'

## CANTO XXIII

While I gazed into the depths of those green leaves,
Trying to see what might be concealed there,
Like one who wastes his weekends in bird hides in Fingringhoe,

The bearded poet called out to me: 'C'mon, man,
We should get moving now. We can spend the time we
Have more usefully than in birdspotting.'

So, I quickly turned about, and just as quickly
Sped up to keep pace with the poets, whose talk was
Such that every step I took was well rewarded.

Then suddenly at my back I hear the strain of
'*Lip up fatty, ah lip up fatty, for the reggae*,' sung
In tones at once joyful and heavy with grief.

'Berrigan, say, what sounds are these I hear?'
I asked, and he replied: 'It's Bad Manners, I think,
Sung by the shades untying the knot of their habits.'

Just as ramblers, absorbed in thought,
When they overtake strangers on the trail,
Greet them without stopping, with a nod of the head,

So, from behind us, moving at a pace,
A band of spirits shot past, silent and determined,
Staring at us with a look of amazement.

The sockets of their eyes were like the gouged hollows
You see in a sculpture by Giacometti,
Their faces were death-pale, and their bodies so wasted

That every gnarled bone protruded beneath the skin.
I doubt that even those Levi described,
As they daily grew closer and closer to death,

Had skin drawn so tight to the bone, or worn so thin.
Even that shadow of a man rescued from the camps by
Marguerite Duras, as she describes in *La Douleur*,

Could not have been more wasted than these souls.
'What exactly is going on here,' I said to Berrigan,
My guide, 'these spirits look like Holocaust survivors,

But surely, if there was a lesson to be learned
From the Holocaust, it was *never again*.
This torment is intolerable –

We can't just stand here and watch, like voyeurs,
Somebody needs to do something about this!'
'I understand where you're coming from,' said Berrigan,

'But you're forgetting where you are. Trust me, these are
Spirits, not living souls, and the pain they feel
Is not the pain you are imagining.'

I was still struggling to come to terms with
The horror I saw around me, not
Understanding its cause, when suddenly

One of the famished souls turned his eyes
Towards me, staring from deep within his skull,
Then cried: 'What an unexpected pleasure!'

I would never have known him by his appearance alone,
But in his still-mellow voice I recognised something
That the features of his emaciated face concealed.

And this spark of recognition rekindled in my memory
The picture of those features now so changed,
And I saw again Hardwood's face.

'Don't worry yourself about the withered scabs
That cover my skin, or the lack of flesh on me now,
We don't get a chance to do Joe Wicks here, you know,'

He began, 'but give me some news from Wivenhoe,
And those two you walk with, tell me who they
Are, and how the Hell did you get up here?'

'Seeing your face at the moment of death,' I said,
'I wept, and now the grief I feel is just as great,
Seeing your face so horribly disfigured.

But tell me what it is that strips you so bare.
Don't ask me to speak, I am speechless,
But speak to me, and take your time, I'm in no hurry.'

And he: 'Essex County Council provided
The machinery whereby the water and the
Tree we have just passed emaciate us so.

And all these people who weep and sing at once,
Like boozers being thrown out at closing time,
Having drunk more than they can handle,

Regain here in hunger and thirst their self-respect.
The chemicals which come from the fruit and
From the spray which is sprinkled over the leaves

Revive in us the craving to eat and drink our fill,
Like that sweet smell that used to come up the
Stairs from the kitchen in the Black Buoy.

As we tread round this featureless terrace
More than once is our pain renewed –
I say pain, but I ought to say pleasure,

For it sets us free from our addictions. It won't
Surprise you if I tell you that there's more
Than one soul from Wivenhoe in rehab here.

And there are a few celebrities here
As well, Amy Winehouse among them –
When I first met her I showed her my poem

About her and she was quite into it,
So if you can ever persuade Bloodaxe to do a
Selection of my poems, you might slip that in.'

And I: 'Hardwood, since the day when you turned
Your back on Wivenhoe for a better life,
Since your last day, less than three years have passed.

How have you climbed so high up the Essex Alp?
I imagined – sorry – that I'd find you down below
Where souls who wasted time must pay with time,

For you were always putting off your projects
To the last, all talk and no action.'
'It was my wife Susan, with her flowing tears,'

He replied, 'who brought me here so soon,
To drink the sweet wormwood of these torments.
She never stopped thinking about me,

And this helped me move on from the slope where
Souls must wait and set me free from those tedious
Rounds. She didn't say any prayers for me,

Of course, we were dyed-in-the-wool atheists,
As you know, but she sped me on with
Tears and conversation and meditation.

And I can tell you, that since my departure, she's
Got even more involved in grass roots activism, and
She's helped set up a new Homeless Centre in Colchester.

The Barbagia of Sardinia that Dante writes about
Are nothing compared to the brainless Essex Girls
That parade up and down that High Street at weekends,

But one or two Essex Girls, who used to like nothing
Better than to get their tits out on a Saturday night,
Though between you and me they were a bit of alright,

She's actually converted to the cause.
They've stopped clubbing, given it up, and now they take
Cups of tea to the homeless camped out in shopfronts.

But tell me about yourself, my friend,
You can see how everyone here, me included,
Is staring there where you block out the sun.'

I answered: 'If you've started reading Dante, as I
Gather from your talk – and I know too from when we last
Spoke on Earth you were growing fond of Pessoa –

The memory of Poetry Wivenhoe, where we
Both cut our teeth, must torture you now.
From that life, and from my teaching duties,

I was called away by the one with the beard
Who leads me here. Still clothed in this flesh
I came through the Infernal Campus

Of the true dead with this poet as my guide.
From there, sustained by his pills, I came up here
Climbing and ever circling round this mount

Which straightens what the world has twisted in you.
He says that I shall have his company
Until we reach where Marina Warner still resides –

And from there I must go without him.
Berrigan (I pointed at him) told me all this himself,
He's an Ex-Visiting Professor at Essex,

The other spirit standing there is he
For whom the mountain's terraces trembled
Just now, he's the poet Tim Atkins, you

Might have seen him read once at Art Exchange?'

## CANTO XXIV

Walking did not slow our talk, nor did talking
Slow our walk, in fact the more we talked
The more we seemed to race along, as if

Fuelled by our breath, like skiffs in a good wind.
And all those shades, who looked like things who had died a
Second time, showed through the turning pits of their eyes

Their sheer amazement at seeing one who was still living.
I picked up where I'd left off, and said: 'Atkins
Is fit, if he's climbing now at a leisurely

Pace, it's on account of Berrigan, my guide –
The last time *he* exercised was when he was
At rehab in New York in the 80s.

But tell me about that bright daughter of yours,
And are there any here that I should know about
Among these shades that are gawping at me?'

'My daughter, who is just as kind as she
Is intelligent, is a lawyer now,
Working with refugees trapped in Calais.'

This he said first, and then: 'As for the shades
Here, I can introduce you to a few of them
By name, for they all have a history,

Even if abstinence has made their features
Indistinguishable to a visitor.
That one' – he pointed to a shade nearby –

'Is the poet Ciaran Carson, from Belfast,
A great scholar, and an even greater drinker,
We tried to get him to read at Poetry

Wivenhoe once, but he'd just had a heart bypass,
The one behind him – can you see that face
Even more withered than the rest? –

Once held in his arms St Mary the Virgin, Wivenhoe,
He was an Arsenal supporter, like me – remember
Thierry Henry? – and he loved a pint with jellied eels.'

Then, as we ambled on, he named many others,
One by one, and none of them seemed the least
Bothered to be picked out from the crowd.

I saw two souls out of sheer hunger chewing
On empty air: the art critic Andrew
Graham-Dixon, and his friend Giorgio Locatelli,

Who toured Italy for the BBC,
Grazing on the culture and the cuisine.
I saw too Phil Tushingham, who I'd once known

In Exmouth, with his single arm stretched out
Towards the tree – on Earth he tried to drink
As much as possible, and with less thirst than here,

Yet no one ever saw him satisfied.
Sometimes, in a bustling street, a face will
Stand out in the crowd, and so it was that

My eyes lit on that shade from Belfast,
Who was edging his way towards me.
I heard him mumble something – something like

'Gráinne' came from his lips, as he pushed across the terrace.
'Poet,' I said, 'do you wish to talk with me?
Then speak up, so I can hear what you're saying.'

'A woman,' he said, 'who lives in Belfast,
One you haven't yet met, or had cause to meet,
Will invite you to read in that strife-torn city,

Hated by all, and give you reason to cherish it.
If my words seem obscure, just remember what
I've said – future events will clarify their sense.

But tell me, do I not see before me
He who rewired those old sonnets with lines like:
"Shall I compare thee to a Smirnoff ad?"

Your work brought something new to Irish poetry,
Showing how a respect for tradition could be
Married to experimental style.'

'I've done nothing special in my work,' I said,
'I'm one who, when a poem comes, listens to
What it has to say and notes it down.

If I've done anything worthwhile, it's because
I'm lucky enough to have met a few good poets
And have learned from them to take what's useful

From any tradition, whether it's John Cage
Or W.B. Yeats, Oulipo or the New York School,
And mix it up into a kind of demotic hybrid.

But that already sounds like theory.
I like people who experiment, for sure,
But I still have ears for quieter and older voices.'

'Friend,' he said, 'you make it sound simple,
But there's something in your style that makes
My own lines look a bit too fancy at times,

And which makes the work of Kennelly
And Montague look a bit too plain.
And nobody who examines closely these

Styles can see the difference more clearly than I can.'
I wasn't completely sure what he was driving at,
But he stopped at that point, pleased with what he'd said,

And spoke no more, as if there was nothing to be added.
Then, as birds that winter along the Stour
Take flight in a single mass from waterlogged fields,

Then, gaining speed, fly in single file –
Just so that mass of shades turned as one,
Then suddenly sped away, light from thinness and desire.

And as a weary runner slows down,
Letting the others pass him by
Till the heaving in his chest subsides,

So did Hardwood let that famished flock
Overtake him, and came on with me behind,
As he asked: 'When do you think we'll hook up again?'

'How long I've got to live I do not know,'
I said, 'but even if I get some terminal illness next month
Or Covid-19 takes me out, my heart will already be waiting

On the shore, for the university where I work
Is being stripped of good day by day
And seems destined, or disposed, to ruin.'

'It's all gone kind of corporate, hasn't it,'
He said, 'it's not what it used to be
When it was known for its radicalism.

But don't despair. Already I see him
Who is most to blame dragged by the tail of a beast
Down to the pockets where the Vice-Chancellors are buried,

With every stride the creature gains speed,
Faster and faster, until it buries him head first,
Feet kicking wildly in the air.

But now I have to leave you, I've rambled on too
Much already, and I've got time to make up
After walking so long at this snail's pace,

And time is precious to us on this terrace.'
As sometimes in a cross-country run, as you near
The finishing post, a runner breaks away and sprints on

To have the honour of the red ribbon,
So he parted from us with a sudden burst of speed,
Leaving me to make my way with those two poets.

When he had raced so far ahead of us
That my eyes could follow him no better than
My mind sometimes followed his rambling words,

I took my eyes from his shape – and suddenly,
Right in the middle of the path in front of me
Another tree appeared, its boughs heavy with fruit.

I saw shades underneath it, raising their hands,
And shouting I don't know what up at the boughs,
Like children who are clamouring for something from

Some negligent carer who refuses to answer their cries
But instead, frustrating them all the more,
Holds up high what they want and doesn't hide it.

At last the souls gave up, and drifted off.
Then we walked right up to that imposing tree
Which says no to all requests, where a notice

By its roots read: DO NOT TOUCH.
'According to the Guidebook,' said Berrigan,
'The tree talks, and every hour, on the hour,

It talks about problems linked to obesity.'
'Let's give that a miss,' said Atkins, 'I'd rather
Walk. What else does it say in the Guidebook?'

'There's a quiz, if you're interested,' said Berrigan.
'What collective name is given to the
Mythological beasts, half-man half-horse,

That are depicted on the Parthenon frieze?'
'Centaurs,' said Atkins. 'And what is the name of the
Slug-like alien in the *Star Wars* franchise,

Known for his insatiable appetite, who
Imprisons Han Solo in carbonite?' 'Jabba,' I said.
So, walking close to the cliff, we answered questions

From the Guidebook, then, walking freely in the open,
Each of us silent and lost in thought,
We had gone a good way past the tree,

When suddenly a voice called out: 'You there, you three
Loners, what heavy thoughts have reduced you to such silence?'
I gave a start like some timid young animal,

Then I raised my head to see who had spoken –
Never in a furnace was there seen
Metal or glass so radiantly red

As was the face of that Alp Angel who said to me:
'If you are looking for the way to climb go no
Farther, this is the path for those who look to burn.'

Though disconcerted by his ruddy looks
I turned around and followed behind the poets,
Letting the words of the Alp Angel direct my climbing boots.

He held out his hand for my card as we
Drew nearer, adding another stamp as I passed.
I felt a breeze strike softly on my brow,

Then we turned and began to climb once more.

## CANTO XXV

Now was the time to climb without delay,
For it was already getting hot on Mersea Island,
While in Colchester, The Bull was filling up

For its socially-distanced barbecue – like New Nature
Writers on a man walk, spurred on by triple book deals
And the pursuit of the Wordsworthian sublime,

We made our entrance through the gap and,
Squeezed by the rocks on either side,
Strode up the stairs in single file.

Fledgling swallows that long to fly, will flutter
Their wings, then, still not bold enough to quit
The nest, let them drop again. I have seen

This countless times on *Springwatch*, and the lesson
Is always the same – just go for it!
Maybe it's because I missed out on a

Public school education, but the question I
Wanted to ask Berrigan just kept turning over
In my mind and I couldn't get it past my chapped lips.

Berrigan, alert as ever, encouraged
Me to speak: 'Spit it out dude!' he said,
Reaching into his jacket for a Chesterfield.

Before he could offer me another pill,
I spoke up: 'How come they're all so wasted,
Since, well, they're shades, aren't they? I mean, surely

They don't actually need to eat in any case?'
Berrigan took a long draw on his Chesterfield,
Then launched on one of his poetic disquisitions:

'You've read Ovid, haven't you?' he said. 'There's a
Character in one of his stories, Meleager
I think, well, when he was born the Fates were

Obviously in a bad mood, for they said to
His mother – I can't remember what she'd done
To piss them off – that his life was only

Going to last as long as a log she'd just put on the fire.
A *log*, get that! Well, she quickly took it off and put it
In a safe place, but then, to cut a long story short,

Eventually she got fed up with Meleager for some
Reason, and so she threw the log back on the fire.
He died at once, painfully. If you think about this story,

Well, it's just the same – sometimes things happen.'
Berrigan must have seen from the look on my face
That I still wasn't convinced, so he carried on.

'If theory's what you want, think of Lacan.
In "The Mirror Phase" he points out how the child
First forms its idea of itself, the ego, when

It sees its reflection in a mirror. Like the
*Ego*, the most fundamental thing we have, is formed by the
Reflection of light off of a mirror?

Now do you see? I can't put it more clearly
Than that, but if you still don't get it we have Atkins
Here, he'll be able to explain better than me.'

'If you want me to explain why the shades
Here are so thin,' said Atkins, 'then I will.
It's not difficult to grasp. Human beings, formed by

Fucking when the ovaries are fertile, as with all
Mammals, begin life as a fetus, which grows into an
Infant, then, given the right kind of nutrition –

Protein for growth, calcium for the bones, and so on –
Eventually it turns into an adult, when it can fuck itself.
Like all creatures, humans have a soul, most of

Them at any rate, though we can all think of exceptions –
Theresa May, Cliff Richard, Carol Ann Duffy, I won't go on.
A lot of breath has been wasted on defining the soul,

But if you think of it as what these people don't have
You're half way there. It's energy, love, motion, though not
Andrew Motion, and it never dies, in fact nothing dies,

Like atoms, things just change into other things,
A kind of constant cycle of recycling – this is
Something else Ovid describes in his *Metamorphoses*,

Which Ted just mentioned. Personally speaking,
My soul was once in a frog, which helps to explain
Why I like Basho so much, though don't get me started

On McCaffery's *Basho Variations*. So,
When a body does what we call dying, which is
Basically a repurposing of atoms,

The soul moves on, and if it lands in the Colne
It goes to Essex University, as everyone knows, whereas
If it lands in the mouth of the Colne it comes here.

And just as the sperm and ovary combining form
A fetus, as we've seen, so the soul and the waters
Of the Colne combine to form a shade.

For as the air, after a downpour,
Is filled with the colours of the rainbow,
Born out of the refracted light,

Just so, the damp air enveloping the soul
Where it has fallen takes on the form
Imprinted by the soul's own karma.

And if the shade isn't to die, so to speak,
For in truth nothing dies as we've seen, or
If the shade isn't to *wither* to put it more clearly,

It must take in energy, just like the human body.
In a word souls need food, that's where the idea
Of "soul food" comes from. Milton is a poet I don't

Warm to much, but read *Paradise Lost*,
He explains it all there at tedious length,
How even angels need some tuck from time to time.

We can speak, even as shades, we can laugh,
And we can shed tears and breathe heavy sighs,
As you must have heard here on this mount.

To put it in a nutshell, it's simply a misconception
That shades don't need to eat – and like you, if they
Don't eat, they waste away. *Quod erat demonstrandum*.'

And now, turning to the right, we had come to
The last torture, and all of our attention
Was taken by what now confronted us:

There the inner bank throws out a wall of flame,
Like a gas jet in a boiler, only bigger,
While a wind whips up from the brink, deflecting

The flames backwards and creating a narrow pathway.
So we had to walk along the exposed side
One by one, in single file, and I feared the

Fire on one side, as much as I was afraid of
Falling down to the shore on the other.
This wasn't a good place to be for someone

Who dislikes the heat and suffers from vertigo.
Berrigan must have seen me hesitating and
Uttered words of encouragement: 'Watch your step!

You need to keep looking down at the path
Beneath your feet, just concentrate on that,
And don't look over the edge – one slip and you're gone.'

Then suddenly I heard, sung out in the very core of the
Furnace: *'Burn baby burn! Let me be your bunsen burner.*
*Burn baby burn! Let me be your naked flame!'*

Which made me want to peer into the heat,
And there I saw spirits walking in the fire,
And so I gazed at them and at my feet,

Now glancing one way, now the other.
When they had finished singing that number
They all chanted out loud: *'No men here!'*

Then launched straight away into another song.
When they had finished they appeared to sit
Down together in a circle and started to tell

Each other stories: one spoke about how
They were groped by their boss at work, one of
How she had gone for six months without sex.

Then they went back to chanting again, then
To singing once more, before they all sat down
Again to tell their stories to each other.

And I think this must go on without a break,
All the time the fire is burning them:
It's by such therapy that they pass their time,

It must, in the end, do them good.

## CANTO XXVI

Along the ledge, now roped together as one,
We made our way, and more than once Berrigan cried out:
'Take care now! Walk only where you see me walk!'

The sun, already lower in the afternoon sky
– Which had the whitish tone of Humbrol Duck Egg Blue –
Was beating down on my right shoulder now,

Throwing one shadow towards the flames, while
The bright light of the flames themselves threw another
Shadow back, towards the brink,

And this double shadow caused many of the shades who
Were now passing us within the flames to stop in
Wonder, and among themselves they began to whisper:

'That one does not look like a spirit.'
Then some of them pressed towards me, as far as they could,
Careful not to step out of the furnace.

'You there, who plod behind the other two,
I'd say you're no idlebones, but walk there
In show of reverence for your companions,

Whoever they might be. Stop and speak to me,
Who burn in thirst and fire. I'm not alone – each of
The shades here would drink up your words with more

Thirst than people struck by famine in Ethiopia.
Tell us, how come you block out the light utterly,
Like a brick wall, as if you had escaped the nets of death?'

So spoke one of them to me – an imposing figure –
And at once I would have answered him, were it not that
In the same instant I was distracted by

A sudden commotion: through the very centre
Of the path of flames a crowd of people appeared
From the opposite direction, and I paused to wonder.

Then, from both sides, the shades could be seen hurrying
On their way, pausing a moment to kiss those they met
On the cheeks, as they do in France, before passing on –

It made me think of the swarms of black ants I
Had seen on David Attenborough, who rush to rub
Their antennae together to exchange information.

Here, as soon as they'd exchanged greetings,
Before taking the next step to depart,
Each group tried to outshout the other:

The ones that had just arrived through the flames
Shouted: 'Oxfam!' And the others who stood
There cried: 'Petticoats up! Trousers down!'

Imagine white egrets forming two flocks: one flies off
Towards Norway, one to the Mediterranean,
One to escape the heat, and one the frost –

So, here, each party went their separate ways,
And all, in tears, took up their separate chants,
With cries of pain and anguish.

Then those same spirits who had first questioned me
Drew close to me as before,
Intent on listening, their faces glowing.

This time, I didn't hold back, but spoke at once:
'Forgive me for not answering you before,
When you put your burning question to me,

And forgive me a second time, for that's
A terrible pun I didn't intend.
I haven't left my limbs back on Earth,

But have dragged them up here with me,
Through the Infernal Campus and to this shore,
With all their aches and pains intact.

I'm scaling this peak for the same reason
You might go to a hospital to get
Your cataracts operated on – to *see*.

There's a woman who won the Holberg Prize,
Who now has a residency on this mountain,
Who sent this bearded poet to rescue me,

And so I drag my mortal parts through your world.
But tell me, so that I may put it in my book, who
Are you, and who is that crowd making off behind you?'

As a mountain goatherd is struck with awe and wonder
When he first enters the city, falling silent
And gawping at all he sees, so were these shades now,

Yet when they had pulled themselves together,
The same soul who had quizzed me before began:
'Good luck to you, traveller, who in these border

Lands of ours hope to find a cargo to ship
Back home so as to find a better death!
These souls that run away from us as I gabble

Committed the offence for which Justin Forsyth,
Once CEO at Save the Children, heard
His staff call him "scumbag" behind his back,

Therefore they run off shouting "Oxfam!", in
Self-reproach, thinking of the girls abused in Haiti,
They use their shame to stoke the flames.

I couldn't tell you exactly what I'm doing here, but it
Wouldn't be unlike that old bastard upstairs to make me
Burn for visiting Rue Saint-Denis with Giacometti.

Whatever we did, following our appetites,
It was not a corporate crime. The words we shout
You'll hear bandied about in the theatre.

It would take too long to tell you who we all are
By name, and I have no inclination to do so.
You'll find here those you'd expect to find here:

Theatre directors, film directors, actors, publicans,
Priests, politicians, lecturers, voice coaches, police
Constables. No surprises there, I'm sure you'll agree.

I can put your curiosity to bed regarding myself, though –
I'm Samuel Beckett, and now I purge myself here
Because I repented well, before the end came.'

Dante writes how as King Lycurgus once
Raged with grief, two sons discovered their lost
Mother and rejoiced – I felt the same to hear

That spirit name himself, father of me
And father of my betters, on whose work
I'd toiled for three years to write a PhD.

I heard no more, I could not speak,
I walked, lost in thought, my eyes fixed on his shade,
Afraid to approach the wall of flames.

At last my eyes were satisfied. Then I spoke:
I told him how once, walking in Paris, I
Had come across him sitting in a café.

That unmistakable mane, shot through with white.
I sat outside on a bench, overawed,
All I could do was sit and stare,

Thinking that's Samuel fucking Beckett!
I didn't dare to go up to him and speak,
And have been longing to do so ever since that moment.

He answered me: 'Was it Le Petit Café
By any chance? It was my favourite. The memory
Of that place even Lethe couldn't take away or make fade.

Alive, I hated "admirers", I never wished
To be admired, only to leave my stain on the silence,
And wake people up to the shit that surrounded them.

But if what you have told me is true,
Tell me why it is – I can see it in your look –
That you put me on such a pedestal.'

And I to him: 'Those grimly funny stories and plays
Of yours, which, for as long as our tongue serves for
Writing, will render precious even the ink you used.'

'Poppycock,' he said smiling, 'I struggled to write
Anything at all in my *mother tongue*,
As you'll know if you've clapped eyes on a copy

Of my *Dream of Fair to Middling Women*,
Which was brought out against my will – that's why
I turned to French in desperation.

But if you like, I can show you one right away
(He pointed to a spirit up ahead) who's been
Called a *better craftsman* in his mother tongue.

Symbolists, Vorticists, writers of long novels – more
Skilled than the lot of them he was! They're fools who think
Your man from Sandymount was a better poet, and let's

Face it, they both barked up the wrong tree in politics.
They judge by reputation alone, their minds made up
Before they pay any attention to art or reason.

Hugo was judged this way in the past – it's always
The Romantics – everyone praised him to the skies,
But who would touch him with a barge pole now?

But enough of that, I've gabbled on plenty.
Just one thing, though, before I go – if you happen
To step inside a church when you're back on Earth

Just say an *Our Father* for me there, to be on the
Safe side, at least the part appropriate for us here,
Who are now delivered from any evil!'

Then, perhaps to make room for others who were near
Him, he disappeared into the fire like a
Fish into the water when it dives to the bottom.

I went forwards a little, towards the shade
He had pointed out, and said that I had
Come to pay homage to the *better craftsman*.

He laughed at that, then began to talk freely:
'You please me so much with your courteous greeting
That I cannot conceal myself, nor would.

I am Ezra, who weep and sing as I go.
With grief I view all my past follies behind me, and
Rejoicing I see the day I long for ahead.

Now, I beg you, by the light that guides you
To the top of the stairway, remember,
In better times, my suffering here.'

Then he hid himself in the fire that refines them.

## CANTO XXVII

It was the hour when the sun would have been at
Its hottest, over Providence, Rhode Island,
Where Berrigan was born, and it must have been

Around six o'clock here, on Mersea Island,
Where the daylight was beginning to fade,
Yet the fierce heat of the flames made it hotter

Here than anywhere on the equator.
Standing on the bank, beyond the reach of
The flames, an Alp Angel appeared to us:

She was wearing a cap, like many of
The guides, but was out of uniform, and
Because of this we could see clearly what

We had not seen before, a pair of wings, like those
Of a swan, protruding from behind the hump of
The shoulders. She was singing softly to herself

'*A good heart these days is hard to find*,' and at first did
Not appear to see us, but when she did
Her voice rang out loud and clear: 'Dear souls,

Who climb this mount to reach the summit,
You can go no further without first
Suffering the fire. So step into the flames,

And listen out to what is sung beyond.'
When I heard these words I felt like a man
Who is about to be burned alive.

As in a panic attack, I broke out in an
Uncontrollable sweat, and as I stepped backwards,
Towards the ledge, staring into the flames, images

Shot through my mind of what human bodies look like
When they are incinerated alive, images
Of the death camps, Ground Zero, Grenfell Tower.

Both my guides approached me, and Berrigan, gripping my
Arm tightly, said: 'This isn't going to be a walk in the
Park, buddy, but sure as Hell it's not going to kill you.

Remember everything we've been through. If I
Saw you through when we rode astride the King of Limbs,
Do you think I'm going to let you down now?

Believe me when I say that if you spent a
Whole semester within the crucible of these
Flames, it would not singe a single hair on your head.

If you still don't believe what I'm telling you,
Try it out for yourself. Take your boots off and
Throw them in – it won't even singe your laces.

So get a hold of yourself, and quit stalling.
Take my hand, come on, we can *do* this!'
But I stood there, frozen, like a statue.

Berrigan gave me one of his looks when he saw
Me fixed there, then said: 'What are you waiting for?
Only this wall keeps you from Marina.'

When Pyramus, about to give up the ghost, heard Thisbe
Utter her name, he raised his blurry eyes and saw
Her standing there, the day mulberries became blood red.

Just so, my recalcitrance melted into air –
Hearing the name which always brings delight
Into my mind, I turned to face my guide.

He shook his head and beamed, as at a child won
Over by a toffee apple, revealing his bad teeth.
'Well then,' he said, 'what are we doing standing here?'

Then, entering the flames ahead of me, and unhitching
The rope that bound us, he asked Atkins, who for some time
Now had been walking between us, to take up the rear.

At Harland and Wolff, in Belfast, I have seen
Vats of molten steel, glowing red with the heat –
Now, as I stepped into the fire, I would

Gladly have submerged myself in one of those vats
To find relief from the intensity of the heat.
Berrigan, my guide, tried to comfort me,

Reminding me who awaited us on the other side:
'I do believe I see her face already!'
From somewhere ahead, a voice was singing,

As if to guide our blind steps, and following
This voice, we at last stepped out of the flames,
Emerging where the ascent begins.

'*It's a long way to the top*,' resounded from
Behind a wall of floodlights so bright,
I was compelled to turn away my eyes.

Then, an Alp Angel appeared, handing out
Bottles of cold water, and damp face cloths
To cool us down. 'The sun is setting now,' she said,

'And night is approaching. I know you must be
Exhausted, but you can't stay here. Hurry,
Before the sun has given up its light.'

The narrow passage cut straight up through the rock,
At such an angle that my body blocked out
The sun's last rays as they fell on my back.

We had not climbed up many of the steps
When we realised that the sun had now set
Because my long shadow had now vanished.

Yet before the colours stretching across the
Expanse of the horizon had melted into one,
And night was in possession of the sky,

Each of us picked a step to bed down on:
The demands of the mountain at once sapped us
Of the strength and of the will to climb.

Like errant psychogeographers, or
New Nature writers, hoping to get
Close to the lives that shepherds once led,

Before sheep and goats were electronically tagged
With NFU apps on mobile phones,
We settled down in ruminating calm,

Quiet in the shade, free from the burning flames.
I was the sheep, watched by his master
Leaning on his staff, they were the shepherds,

Shut in by walls of stone, this side and that,
At one with nature and with their gods,
Meditating on the mystery of the mount.

Beyond the walls of stone little was visible,
But looking up I could see the stars,
Larger and brighter than they appear to us.

While staring up at them, Berrigan handed
Me some weed, then sleep overcame me –
Sleep which often brings understanding.

At just about the hour when Venus rises,
Followed by the sun, as Beckett writes,
I dreamed I saw a young girl in a meadow,

Picking wild flowers, and she spoke these words:
'I am Leah, I spend my days weaving
Garlands of meadow flowers with my hands.

My sister Rachel sits by her mirror, never moving.'
I was wondering what to make of this, having
No clue, when Berrigan too stepped into my dream,

A Chesterfield in one hand, the Guidebook in the other.
'Lookee here,' he said, 'it's all in the Guidebook:
That dame with the flowers and shit, Leah,

She's kind of a *doer* – like that suffragette
Who threw herself under the King's horse.
Her sister Rachel's more of a *contemplative*,

And in that sense more like the suffragist
Millicent Fawcett, who was opposed to violent protest.
Their story's in the Bible, but it boils down

To this: the active life and the contemplative.
It's one of those things Yeats worried about – for us
Poets it's a question of getting the right balance.

Maybe that's something Ginsberg achieved, he
Was a contemplative alright, but he always
Mucked in when he thought it would make a difference.'

And now, with the brightness of dawn,
The shadows of night were fleeing on every side,
And my sleep and my dream with them; I got up,

To join the poets who had already risen.
'We thought you'd never wake up,' said Berrigan,
'Don't tell me you've been dreaming again? This is your big day!

Marina is waiting to greet you up ahead.'
Something like that Berrigan must have said
To me, it's hard to remember exactly,

For I was suddenly so full of a desire
To reach the summit, that at every step
I took I felt myself grow lighter.

Once the stairs, swiftly climbed, were all behind us,
And we were upon the topmost step,
Berrigan turned to me, fixing me with his stare:

'This is it, dude, you've seen the temporal
And the eternal fire, and now we're at that place
Where I'm surplus to requirements.

I bust a gut to get you here, and the going
Was tough – this old mule now needs to take a
Back seat, putting it bluntly, you're on your own.

The steep paths are far below, now you can
Feel the sun on your brow, and feast your eyes
On the grass and the trees that grow at this height.

Until those lovely eyes come into view,
Which, full of tears, once urged me to come to you,
You can rest here, and walk about as you please.

Don't expect any more guidance from me – you
Don't need it. You know why you've come here, and
You know what you want. So farewell, it's been a blast,

I crown and mitre you lord of yourself!'

## CANTO XXVIII

Now eager to see for myself the
Ancient woodland thick with reflected greens,
Which made the daylight softer to the eye,

Without messing about I left the bank
And made my way across the ground whose dark
Redolent soil gave a tangy fragrance to the air.

My sweaty forehead felt the stirring of cool air,
Whose flow was steady and unchanging,
Striking no harder than the gentlest breeze,

And, in this constant current of cool air, each branch
With dancing leaves was bending to one side
Towards where the Essex Alp first casts its shadow;

Yet they did not bend so sharply towards the ground
That the nightingales amongst the lower branches and
Scrub could not continue to run through their sets:

In full-throated ease they welcomed
The first breezes within the leaves which
Accompanied their song in a windy drone –

Like the sound Dante heard passed from branch to
Branch in the pine forest on the shore of Chiassi
When Aeolus set free Sirocco winds.

By now, although I walked slowly, I found
Myself so deep within the ancient woodland
That I could no longer make out where I had come in,

Then all of a sudden I saw, blocking the way,
A stream whose lapping waters nourished the wild
Garlic that sprouted in profusion along its bank.

The clearest of all streams on our planet, those in
The Swiss Alps or at Centre Parks in Whinfell Forest,
Are muddy cesspools compared to this,

Whose depths hide nothing, though it flows
Beneath perpetual shade, where the light
Of the sun and the moon scarcely penetrates.

I was forced to stop, but that didn't stop my eyes
From gazing in wonder across that stream
At the fresh boughs and flora bursting into life,

And then I saw – when I had stopped gawping
At the endless carpet of bluebells, which looked like
A forest scene from *The Ladybird Book of Nature* –

A solitary figure at work there, who did not
Seem interested in picking flowers, but noted
With care the identity and location of

Every specimen that grew beneath the trees.
She was wearing headphones and singing along
To a tune I could not hear, though the words

'*Try! Try!*' echoed across the stream and into my ears.
Something about the scene reminded me of the time,
In Belfast, when we'd gone mossing on a

Grassy bank by the Lagan, not far from Drumbeg.
She hadn't yet seen me, and I didn't want to
Alarm her, but I saw no alternative

But to start moving my arms about to attract
Her attention, trying to put on my friendliest face,
Hoping that even if I looked like an idiot,

She would at least twig that I wasn't a paedophile.
Looking a little suspicious at first,
She at last raised her face to where I was standing.

'I'm a visitor,' I said, holding up my pass, 'I've come
Here through the flames with my two guides, who are
Just behind me, to learn the secrets of the mount.

Would you mind stepping a bit closer to
The stream, so that we can talk a little?'
Just as a woman practicing Aikido

Will turn, keeping her feet together on the ground,
One in front of the other, hardly moving,
So she, among the sea of bluebells,

Turned round towards me and, snapping off her
Headphones, made her way towards the stream,
Where, without talking, she raised her eyes to mine.

Smiling, she stood there on the opposite bank,
Saving the data on her tablet on which she had
Logged the flora that grew in this habitat.

The stream kept us only six feet apart, but
The Hellespont, where Byron showed off his front crawl,
Was no less hated by Leander than this ditch by me.

'I'm guessing you're all new to this place,' she started,
'But you've probably heard of the Eden Project. You're
Unlikely to hear Elton John here, but otherwise

The two sites have a lot in common, and in the
Staff room you'll sometimes hear this place called Eden East.
Basically, we function as a kind of world seed bank,

And this sector consists of four hundred acres
Of ancient woodland. I'm happy to show you round,
So if you have any questions, don't hold back.'

'The overflowing stream (which to me suggests it must
Rain here) and the constant breeze,' I began,
'Don't quite fit what I've been told about the mount.'

'If you've been told it never rains here,' she said,
'That's crap, but let me explain some of the key
Factors controlling the microclimate at this height.

We all know storms are common at sea
(Caused by the evaporation of water
Drawn upwards by the heat of the sun),

And to prevent these storms disturbing the
Seedlings in the garden, the architects of this
Island have artificially regulated the climate.

For one thing this mount was constructed to rise
Sufficiently high above sea level that past
The security gate storms are very unlikely.

Which isn't to say they're impossible –
Climate is nothing if not unpredictable.
However, you still get winds up here, but the

Effects of these are ameliorated by the dense
Woodland, which acts as a natural wind break, converting
The air currents into a constant breeze, as you've seen,

Which makes the dense leaves of the forest sing.
And every plant so moved makes the pure air pregnant with
Its seeds which, then, the whirling scatters everywhere.

All lands across the globe conceive and bring to flower the
Different plants endowed with different characteristics,
According to climate and soil conditions.

If the gardeners of Essex knew what you know now,
Nobody would be at all surprised to see a plant
Spring up in their garden where no seeds were sown.

And clock that the seed banks that we keep elsewhere
On the mount are rich in every species, even those
Extinct plants that can no longer be found naturally.

One of our latest projects, which has UN funding, is
To reintroduce these species – like Downy Hemp-nettle –
Into the wild, in protected locations across the country.

The water source here is part of the secret of
Our success. Not only is the water here free from
Pollutants, but it springs from a source that

Doesn't require a system of pumps and conduits,
As with the streams and rivers that farmers exploit
On Earth, that lose then gain their force:

It issues from a natural spring engineered
To give a constant flow which is continually
Replenished by a twin source on two sides.

The water here on this side flows with such power
It can, under laboratory conditions, erase
Bad memories; and on that side, similarly,

The memory of good things can be restored.
It is called Lethe here, on this side, and on the
Other Eunoë. Science can't explain these powers,

But they work, so long as Lethe's waters are taken first.
The sweet taste of both has no equal – not even
Perrier or San Pellegrino come close.

I've talked a lot, and forgive me if I've rambled on
A bit, but even if your thirst is now quenched,
Let me share one further thought with you, which

Has come up in the staff room, it might interest you.
One of our interns, from the Wild Writing MA
At Essex, has been writing a blog where they argue

That the poets of the pastoral tradition –
They pay particular attention to the
Work of Theocritus – in imagining

Arcadia, were dreaming on Parnassus of just such
A place as this – a place of eternal spring where
Every fruit and herb blossoms without labour.'

As she spoke these words, I stole a glance at the two
Poets behind me: and I saw, still lingering,
The smile her final words had brought to their lips.

Then I turned back again to face her gaze.

## CANTO XXIX

Once she had said these last few words she put
On her headphones again and began to
Sing along: '*The only way is up, bay-bee!*'

Seeing her begin to sway, I couldn't help
Thinking of those nymphs that inhabit forest
Glades in mythology – the ones you find

Jumping out from behind every stanza in Spenser –
And as I thought like this I began to think
Too how these fictional nymphs, representing

The sentient life of the forest, were
Not so ridiculous as I'd sometimes felt,
For weren't they an ancient way of saying

How forests were living communities,
How trees communicate with each other,
Which science has since proved true in

The way trees share nutrients and information
Via underground mycelial networks which
To all intents and purposes resemble brains?

She moved against the flow of the stream,
Along the bank – and I followed her, shortening
My steps to match hers. We'd gone no more than

A hundred steps between us, when the banks
Of the stream turned in parallel, so that I must
Have been facing out to sea where the sun rises.

When we had gone a little farther on,
She stopped, then turning towards me said:
'Are you ready for Magic Puffin?'

Suddenly a bright light swept through the wood
On all sides, illuminating the tree canopy
And bouncing off the water in the stream –

At first I took it for a lightning flash,
But lightning goes as quickly as it comes,
And what I saw didn't go, but intensified

As we continued to advance. And then,
As loud music drifted through the luminous
Atmosphere, it suddenly clicked that these

Were lasers cutting through the air,
And as we stepped out into a clearing,
A band was pumping out music on a small stage

In front of an ecstatic crowd. It was The Fall,
And as we pushed our way through the wizard cloaks
I saw Mark E. Smith rip the microphone

From its stand and sing those immortal words:
'*It's the lay of the la-and, my son!*
*It's the lay of the laa-aaand, my son!*'

I'm no dancer, but this was enough to get
Even me going. We started jumping up and down
As if we'd just invented the pogo,

Singing along to each word as Smith steered
The song to its relentless climax. I can't
Remember the whole set – it's a bit of a blur –

But they followed with 'Fiery Jack', 'Cruiser's Creek',
And 'Hark the Herald Angels Sing', each song
Taking us to new heights. At one point Berrigan

Slipped me a pill, and I was off. Moving
In a blissful trance to these first fruits
Of the New Wave, gagging for more to come,

The air, beneath green boughs, became transformed
Before our eyes into a blazing light, and now it
Seemed as if even the trees were singing along,

And waving their leaves and their branches in
Rhythm to the music. Then, before the crowd,
And the trees, and the Earth itself had finished

Their thunderous applause, it was into the next song:
*Bum-bum-pa-dum, bum-bum-pa-dum, bum-bum-pa-dum,*
*Bum-pum, bum-pum…'I drank a ja-aar of coffee,*

*And then I took some of these!'* We were away,
Floating through the air like Uriah Heep
On LSD, and nothing could bring us down.

Oh Oulipo, New York School, beat poets,
Language poets, Dada, Black Mountain College,
Anyone who's out there, even you muses,

Daughters of synchronicity, help me now,
Let Helicon pour forth its streams for me,
And let Alan Halsey help me with his choir

To put in verse things difficult to grasp.
A little farther on, I saw what appeared
To be seven golden poplar trees – a

Distortion caused by the distance and the drugs –
But when I had come close enough to them to
See clearly what they were the still functioning parts

Of my brain identified the shapes as candlesticks,
And I heard the words *Om Ah Hum* in a chant.
Above the polished gold shone a brilliant light,

Brighter than moonlight in a cloudless sky.
Full of bewilderment, I gyrated round
To Berrigan my guide. His answer was

The vacant stare of a man totally tripped out.
Then I turned back to gaze at those high things
Moving towards us as though they did not move –

They moved more slowly than the Brexit negotiations
Led by Theresa May. Then at my shoulder our
Female guide cried: 'Why are you so hung up on those

Fucking candles? Don't you want to see what comes behind?'
Then, on a float, I saw a group of musicians
Sitting cross-legged, playing drums and flutes and sitars,

All were clothed in garments supernaturally white.
I saw the slender flames as they advanced
Leaving the air behind them painted with colours –

Like the tricolour painted on the sky by
The jet fighters flying over the Champs-Elysées
To celebrate France's win in the World Cup.

Under that trippy sky we heard the sitar
Of Ravi Shankar slowly come into focus
As his fingers danced up and down the frets.

Accompanied by his daughter Anoushka he
Played a mournful love song, and as they moved
On we heard the words: '*I am missing you,*

*Oh Krishna, where are you?*' breeze through the
Air, accompanied by flutes and bells and drums.
When once this float had passed slowly by,

As groups of stars will replace other stars
High in the heavens, following them there came
Another float, this one packed with young refugees

From all over Africa, who were
Enacting scenes from *The Epic of Gilgamesh*.
One character wore a dark blue cloak

Decorated with gold sequins, another
Wore a crown on his head of forest green,
And they were wrestling together like prize

Fighters in a ring. Among the characters
Milling about on the back of the float was an
Old man with a beard and a beautiful goddess

And puppets of snakes and wild cats and
Scorpion people flanked by a great golden bull,
Its wings decorated with lapis lazuli.

Reader, I can't use up more verses now
Describing them, for I have other needs
Constraining me, here I must spare my words –

But you can read N.K. Sanders' translation
If you don't know the story, or David
Ferry's if you prefer one in verse, and

If you want to see for yourself the winged Bull of
Heaven you can visit the Louvre or go to
The collections in the British Museum.

Behind this float, which bore on its banner
The name *Giocherenda* – you can check out
Their Facebook page – there were three dancers

Circling in a ring near the rear wheels of the truck,
Their heads and their bodies lit up by
Plastic tubing filled with phosphorescent liquid;

One glowed bright red, so red she would hardly
Have been visible in fire, the second looked as if
Her flesh and bones were fashioned out of emerald;

While the third had all the whiteness of new-fallen snow;
At moments the white one led the dance, leaping
And pirouetting as if in a psychotic trance,

At moments the red one took the lead, and from the
Song she sang the others took the tempo of their dance.
Behind this group there followed a troupe of

Fire-eaters dressed in wizard's robes and pointed
Hats, led by a man with a long grey beard
And a rubber mask with three purple eyes.

Behind these dancers and fire-eaters came
A group of half a dozen people on stilts,
Towering high above the crowd, and each wore

A giant papier mâché puffin head, and on
Their backs, blowing in the breeze, scissored capes
Stuck all over with black and white feathers.

Then came a miscellaneous bunch of jugglers
And poets and performers and hangers-on making
Up the rear – one of them rode a penny farthing

And wore a face mask beneath a tricorn hat, another
Was doing an impression of Bruce Forsyth in the
Pose he used to strike for The Generation Game,

And laughing and joking and smoking a
Cigarette I could make out, taller than the rest,
The unmistakable profile of Dr John Cooper Clarke.

There may have been more, I forget, and I
Was still under the influence of the drugs,
But when the group on stilts was directly

Opposite me, and we were separated
Only by the clear waters of the stream,
The whole cavalcade came to an abrupt halt,

From the candles at the front to the poets at the rear.

## CANTO XXX

Where the procession came to a sudden
Halt there were seven tents in a ring, or
Rather in a kind of horseshoe shape,

Pitched snugly up against the bank of the stream
(Just as in a settlement built in a river
Valley the houses will follow the river's course).

An eighth tent, off to one side, had a long queue
Stretching back into the trees, where day trippers and
Performers from the outside had their vaccine passports

Checked, and those without documentation were offered
Covid tests, before they were allowed to join the party.
In the foreground, the group of puffins on stilts continued

To wave their feathers about, then, all of a sudden, one
Of them shouted 'Roll up for the *LRB* Tent!' three times,
And all the other voices on stilts followed hers.

As at last orders all the drunks
Will rise out of their graves, ready to raise
A glass, singing 'Hallelujah!'

Just so rose up above the papier mâché puffins
A hundred angels soaring on their muscular
Wings as high as children on space cakes,

All shouting: 'Not to be missed for anything!'
While tossing a rain of flowers in the air,
Like something from an early Genesis gig.

Sometimes, as day approaches, I have seen
All of the sunshine coast a glow of rose,
The surface of the sea perfectly calm,

As the sun's face rose in a misty veil
Of stratus fractus that enabled the eye
To look straight at it without blinking:

Even so, behind a nebula of flowers
That flowed upwards from angels' hands and then
Poured down on the roof and round the entrance

Of the *LRB* Tent, I saw within,
Seated on a low stage, a lady – she
Wore horn-rimmed spectacles and had her hair

Tied back in a neat bun above a
Vivienne Westwood dress – and instantly
(Though it was some time since I'd last seen her,

And many years since we'd worked together
At Essex, before the transformation)
My soul, that yet could not see her perfectly,

Still felt, succumbing to her mystery
And power, the strength of its enduring love.
No sooner were my eyes struck by the force

Of the high, piercing intellect I had known
From working with her on Memory Maps,
Than I turned to my left – with all

The confidence that makes a child run to
Its mother's arms when overcome with fright
Or joy – to say to Berrigan, my guide:

'It's Marina!' But Berrigan had gone,
He must have slipped off, on a high, into the crowd.
Alone, I pushed my way into the tent, past the

Security guards and their temperature guns, to catch some
Of the action. There was a woman in an *LRB* T-shirt,
At first I didn't recognise her, but as I edged my way

To the front, past disgruntled wizards and climbers sitting
On cushions on the ground, I recognised
The Essex Book Festival Director, Ros Green.

I didn't catch the question she'd put to
Marina, but from the response I guessed
It had been something about her days at Essex.

'Well,' said Marina, 'I'm afraid I'm rather
Weary of going over that story. I've tried
To put it all behind me recently.

The man who took over Essex when I
Was there had worked in National Security,
And had a background in ballistics.

His management style, like the architecture there,
Was brutalist, and approached universities
As businesses, which of course they are not.

At first I thought we were just very unlucky,
But the more I looked into it the more it
Became clear this was a sector-wide problem,

Promoted directly by Government policies.
Stefan Collini has written well about this:
Universities, he says, always seen as troublesome

By policymakers, were handed over to
The Department of Business under the Blair
Government. Yes, it's unbelievable, isn't it?

This brought with it targets and the need to
Be useful to the business sector –
Employability and the rest of it.

It also promoted competition,
Pitting academic against academic,
Which has been deeply damaging.

Combined with the inevitable funding cuts to
The Arts, this reduced academics to the state of
Levi's internees, fighting over a spoon.

I don't want to go over my personal story here –
Suffice it to say that this was an
Environment where I no longer fitted in.'

'More recently,' said Ros, 'you've been working
With refugees in Italy, under the
Banner of Stories in Transit. Can you

Tell us a little about this project?'
'Well, in 2014 I was lucky enough
To be the recipient of the Holberg Prize,

And I wanted to do something with this money.
I was invited to Palermo by Valentina
Castanega, who had been doing a PhD

On my work, and this is where it all began.
This work, as you know, is with migrants.
Some of these boys – and mostly they are boys,

For reasons I won't go into now – have fled conflict zones,
But others are just fleeing *pour l'aventure*.
What these boys get if they're lucky enough

To be given refugee status before they
Fall into the hands of the Mafia
Is clothes, a phone, an ID card, food, a bed.

But what no organisation offers them
Is a sense of belonging to a culture.
These kids come from a rich culture of joking

And dancing and singing and telling stories.
We try to reconnect them to this by
Telling stories with puppets and so on.

We're not interested in refugee stories as such –
There are other organisations who are – but almost
The opposite, in nurturing their imagination.

These people are often very gifted imaginatively.
And without imagination their lives can be
Reduced to a series of perfunctory utilitarian chores.'

'I suppose,' said Ros, 'in a way, that links
Back to what you were discussing earlier, the
Chrestomathic university, as it has been called.'

'Yes,' said Marina, 'it does, and it's something
We need to be on our guard against. This is
Where the Arts, today, still have a crucial role.'

'Well,' said Ros, 'I think we just about have
Time for a few questions. Yes, the man in the red
Climbing hat standing by the inflatable puffin.'

'What's the politics?' he asked. 'I work with refugees
In North London, we do murals and things.
I live in the same council flats as they do,

Which makes the experience more organic.
We don't just drop in for a quick fix, your
Scheme sounds like a parachute organisation.'

'Well, you could call it a parachute organisation,'
Said Marina, 'but there's no other practical
Way for us to engage with these boys,

And besides, people forget that a parachute
Is there to prevent a fatal fall – a
"Chute", as in Albert Camus' famous novel

*La Chute* (from which, incidentally, Mark E.
Smith took the name of his band, The Fall,
Who are appearing at this festival).'

By this point I had made my way right to
The front of the audience, and the bouncers
Were starting to eye me suspiciously,

As if I might be some terrorist or something.
Then, suddenly, Marina spotted me:
'Look!' she said to Ros, 'it's Phil, there in the front row.

Phil, *hallllloooo!* Do come up on stage,
You can tell us about your experience
Of Palermo, as well as of Essex,

Which Ros has just been talking about!'
I wished I'd hung back a bit, but by this point it
Was too late, so, embarrassed, I made my way onto the stage –

All of a sudden the bouncers were my friends –
And sat down between the two of them. 'Tell us,'
Said Marina, 'your experiences of Palermo –

Did you know the Giocherenda were here?'
'Yes,' I said, 'I saw their *Gilgamesh* float, it's amazing!
For me, well, the experience of working in

Palermo was fantastic, and I have to say I
Can't imagine anyone but you pulling it off.
I mean, who else could gather together a team of

Poets and directors and scriptwriters and artists
And musicians and puppet-makers, to start with?
I did find things chaotic at times, and it's hard

Working in so many languages, most of which you
Don't know, but through sheer enthusiasm and goodwill and
Imagination we always managed to pull things off.

Some people warned us off even trying to attempt
A staging of *Gilgamesh* on the last visit,
But together we did actually pull it off. Twice.

And people loved it. It even got a write up in the
*Giornale di Sicilia*, as you know.' I caught
The corner of Ros's eye at this point,

And saw her tap her wrist, indicating we
Were close to time, so quickly wound up by
Saying what a pleasure it had been to

Be involved and how I'd always found working
With Marina Warner inspiring, and how I hoped
That following any interruptions caused by

The coronavirus pandemic things would be able
To pick up again. Then Ros,
Catching my eye again, unexpectedly asked:

'Wasn't it on your watch that Essex lost Marina?'

## CANTO XXXI

I sat before her paralyzed, confused,
I opened my mouth, my throat striving to speak,
But not a single breath of speech escaped.

'It's true, isn't it,' she pressed, 'that you were
In charge when Marina was forced to quit?'
I felt as I often do at a conference

When some arsehole hits you with a question
Out of the blue and you've no idea how to respond.
Yet at such moments the mind takes over on

Automatic pilot, the lips start moving even
If you've no idea what words will come out –
And you sit there, stiffly, watching the drama unfold

As if you were nothing more than a distant bystander.
'Well,' I heard myself say, 'not exactly.'
And I fumbled on: 'Technically the Head

Of Department at the time was Jonathan
Lichtenstein, but there was some bad shit flying
Around, and what with one thing and another

I did get involved. I was bound to, in a way,
As I'd worked more closely with Marina
Than anyone. I did all I could, as did

Some other colleagues, like Karin Littau,
Who were brave enough to stick their necks out.
But you sensed that things weren't going to work out.

To cut a long story short the VC had
Changed his mind about letting Marina have
Time off to judge the Man Booker International,

And it became impossible for her to
Deliver her teaching and do this at the same time.
But you could sense an unacknowledged hostility

In the air. I wasted my breath trying to
Tell the story to management as it was –
I think they told me I was "passive aggressive"

For my pains, a business term I'd never heard
Before, one the Nazis might have used to describe
Their victims had they had it at their disposal.'

Then, turning to Marina, Ros asked her:
'Is there anything you'd like to add about this
Period, it must have been very difficult for you?'

'Yes, if you must. Well, what Philip says is absolutely
True. And there was certainly hostility involved,
Against the whole Department. Looking back now, it

All started at a staffing meeting the VC asked me to
Attend. The case of a post-doctoral student
Came up – he hadn't hit his research output

Targets, and the VC wanted his contract
Terminated. But when we looked into the
Details of the case, it turned out that his

Research supervisor, a professor in the
STEM subjects who he was working under,
Had been ill for some time, and it struck me

That to think of terminating his contract
In such circumstances was deeply unfair.
When I raised this, a number of other professors

Agreed, so we decided to give him a second chance.
The Vice-Chancellor wasn't pleased by this,
But his reaction took even me by surprise.

After this I became the target of his PA –
She kept phoning me in the middle of classes,
Or when I was halfway through a lecture,

For no ostensible purpose beyond making
Me feel unwelcome. They were very careful
Not to leave any trace of this, which is why

They targeted me by phone. There wasn't
A single email, for example, just endless calls,
Asking me if I was available for

Various meetings which never materialised.
Then I was hassled about my availability
For teaching, when they knew I was tied up.

The VC had even congratulated me
When I was asked to chair the Man Booker
International, for it brought prestige to

The university. But now all this goodwill
Went up in smoke, and I was required to fulfil
My teaching commitments like anybody else.

In the end, as you can imagine, I got
Fed up with it all. That's when I resigned.
And when I wrote my piece for the *LRB*.'

'Well,' Ros laughed, 'we all remember *that!*
But I'd like to ask Phil about how the
Department coped after your departure.

Losing Marina must have been a massive blow,
How did the Department deal with this,
And were there reprisals from management?'

'Well,' I said, 'at the time I'd have said not,
At first things just went quiet for a bit.
It happened just before summer, for one thing.

But when we came back in the Autumn term,
We did start to feel the pressure in new ways.
As usual, we fell short of our recruitment quota

In clearing, though this time we'd been set up
To fail with overambitious targets, all part of
The university's programme of expansion.

Subsequently, we were dragged over the coals
With other failing departments, like History,
And told to come up with a *recruitment strategy*.

Dutifully, we pulled out all the stops,
And things went smoothly for a bit, until one day
I was asked for a coffee with the Deputy VC.

He didn't mince his words: it had been decided
At an Estates Management meeting that
LiFTS was to be moved to the former Business

School – Business itself was moving into a
New flagship building – so that refurbishment
Could take place to create a new state-of-the-art

Space for Student Support and Sport Science.
My job was to get the Department on board.
The building in question was a soulless block

Designed by a local building firm that to all
Intents and purposes looked like a branch of HSBC.
Needless to say I wasn't keen:

We were being asked to leave a historic building
Where the likes of Tom Raworth had trod the
Corridors joking with John Barrell.

And to add insult to injury we
Were being asked to move into the former
Home of the Business School – it was a

Deliberate and cynical tactic to uproot
Us from our history and bully us into
Remoulding ourselves along business lines.

At first I was fired up by a spirit of
Resistance, and I protested. But our protests
Fell on deaf ears – if we didn't move we'd

Be offered a suboptimal solution,
And life would become very difficult for us.
At a crisis meeting the Deputy VC

Asked us what the exit strategy was.
I said: "You can either take the door like
Everybody else or self-defenestrate."

Fortunately he laughed, but the game was up.
Briefly we considered the option of chaining ourselves
To the railings, and organising sit-ins,

But re-enacting the 70s wasn't going to cut any mustard.
We moved, but it didn't stop there. Audits
Followed, restructurings, and curriculum reviews,

All of which gradually wore us down and brought us to heel.
Thinking back now on what happened after
Marina left, I'm filled with a sense of regret,

A feeling I could have done more, could have been
More outspoken against this insidious business mentality,
For universities are not businesses,

And so-called business models have no place here.
But when that's all you hear day in and day out
The siren voices gradually break your resistance,

And your ideals end up on the scrap heap.'
We'd now gone well over time, and the audience
Was beginning to drift off. Ros rounded things

Up quickly with some brief words, there were applause,
Then we left the stage by a back entrance.
When we stepped outside, Marina said: 'If recalling

Your time at Essex causes you so much grief, you
Must learn to put it all behind you. The past
Can't be changed. Now, raise your beard and look at me.'

I'd quite forgotten that I'd grown a beard
During the long climb – and I hoped she didn't think
I was trying to pass myself off as a hipster,

For there was mischief in her words.
Yet when I raised my head she was smiling,
And behind her, seated on crates, I saw

The Alp Angels, who had folded their wings
And were now having a quiet smoke.
Then, when I turned my unsure eyes once more,

I saw that Marina was staring me in the face:
'I hope you've had the sense to give up,' she said.
Her words stung me, and all of a sudden

I felt weak at the knees, the climb, all my
Strange encounters, and now, after all this time,
Meeting Marina again, my greatest inspiration,

All caught up with me, it was too much.
I must have fainted – what happened then is known
Only to her who was the cause of it.

When I revived, the woman I first saw strolling
Alone through the woodland was now bending over me,
Saying: 'Hold on to me, hold tight now.' She had

Immersed me in the stream up to my neck,
And now drawing me along she glided across
The stream, towards the bank, with practiced ease.

Before I reached the grassy bank I heard
'*Asperges me!*' – so sweetly sung, my mind
Cannot remember, far less words retell.

The naturalist, opening her arms,
Embraced my head and dipped it in the stream
Just deep enough to let me take a gulp.

Then she lifted me from the waters, cleansed
Of my business mindset, and led me into
A crowd who were dancing in the moonlight.

Among the crowd were the three dancers I
Had seen before, their red, white and green
Phosphorescence whirling in the darkness;

They came towards me, raising their arms to
Join hands above my head, and inviting me
To take part in the dance. I hated dancing

As a rule, but the waters of Lethe
Must have erased more than my business mindset
For I joined in without hesitation trying to remember

Some of the steps Scott Thurston had once shown me.
As we danced to the rhythms that pulsed through
The trees, I saw Marina too whirling to the dance,

And as I looked into her clear eyes I
Saw reflected there, like sunlight in a mirror,
The lasers that were flashing among the trees,

As she stood there unchanged, changing constantly.

## CANTO XXXII

I fixed my eyes on hers, as if in a trance,
As she continued to whirl her arms to the music,
Casting on my eyes her familiar spell,

Then suddenly my gaze was pulled away by the
Three dancers who began to mock me: 'It's rude to stare!'
I heard them shout, sticking their tongues out,

And as I twisted my head towards them
I was like one who had strained his eyes
By looking at the sun with the naked eye,

For so intense had been the light of the lasers
Reflected in Marina's clear eyes
That for an instant I was left blind.

When I had grown accustomed to the dim light –
Dim light, I mean, compared to that effulgence
Which had been burning my retina –

I saw that the procession that had passed us before
Had wheeled about and was now moving back
In the opposite direction, towards the woods.

The dancers took their place behind one of the floats,
The giant puffins followed in the rear,
Their feathers ruffled in the constant breeze.

Atkins and I, along with the naturalist
Who had pulled me across the stream, now walked
Behind the float occupied by the Giocherenda,

Where now two of their number, a man and a woman,
Were acting out a masque relating the lives of
Saint Benedict and Saint Rosalie of Palermo,

Accompanied by violins and percussion.
When they finished, and the drums came to a stop,
I heard the name Adam spoken in the crowd,

Though whether he was one of the performers
Or one of the drummers or string players I cannot tell.
As we walked on through that high wood, we saw

Bright lights hanging in the trees, and as we
Drew closer we saw that these came from LED
Screens hanging from the boughs, displaying video art.

When we had gone about three times the distance
You can throw a frisbee with a strong arm we
Stopped under a tree to gaze up at one of the screens.

It showed an African boy standing on a hill on the
Outskirts of Palermo, beneath the branches of an
Ancient tree, planted long ago by Saint Benedict.

The boy was talking to the camera, in English,
Explaining how he had travelled through Libya
To find a boat to take him to Europe.

He spoke matter-of-factly about the prison
Where he had been detained, fed only on biscuits
And water, where he'd been beaten every day.

He spoke of how he'd worked on a building site
To save money for the crossing and how the
Men he paid had taken his money and vanished.

And he spoke of his home in Nigeria, of
How his stepfather had abused him, and how
One day instead of going to school he left forever.

Now he'd found work in Palermo, as a chef,
At a restaurant called Moltivolti – the hours
Were long, but it was work, and he was free.

When the screen went blank we moved on to a
Small clearing where a number of striped deckchairs
Had been laid out round the trunk of a huge oak,

In the branches of which another film was already
Running. It showed what looked like a collective farm,
I could not make out where it was located,

Perhaps some backwater of the United States,
Or in South America, it was hard to tell;
A woman was talking about domestic abuse,

The penurious wages of farm labourers,
And the right to food. From what I could gather,
The farm had been set up so people could

Work together to grow their own crops,
Working collectively in their spare time
And taking home what they needed to eat.

There was some footage of the land before
They had cultivated it, which was barren and rocky,
Like a piece of abandoned waste ground.

Yet just as the trees on Earth in early spring
Begin to swell, bursting into bloom and
Renewing the colour that was formerly theirs,

Just so, that farm whose earth had been so barren
Renewed itself, and bloomed with colours
Of gold and green and yellow and purple.

The camera showed a group of women sitting
Round a camp fire at night, sharing food and wine,
And as they ate they started to sing.

I did not recognise the song they sang,
For it was not a song we know on Earth,
But then, I did not listen to the end.

Could I describe how the eyes of Argos
Were lulled to sleep by the sad tale of Syrinx –
Eyes that payed so dear for their fruitless watch –

As a painter painting from his model, I would
Try to tell you how I nodded off in the deckchair.
But let those who can paint sleep paint sleep!

I shall only tell you how I awoke:
Someone was shaking me, and a voice was
Calling me: 'What are you doing? Get up!'

And then I woke, to see bent over me
The naturalist who, earlier on, had been
My guide along the banks of the stream.

Worried, I cried out: 'Where is Marina?'
Then she said: 'Look, she's sitting over there
On the tree's roots beneath the newborn leaves.'

I don't know if she said more than this,
For now I'd caught sight of Marina again
I was eager to be by her side.

She sat there on the earth, alone, and said:
'Now, for those who still talk of business models,
Watch this video well, and what you see

Put into writing when you have returned.'
Then I, obediently, at the feet of her
Commands, gave mind and eye to satisfying her.

The video installation I then watched told
A sorry story, for it displayed a satellite chart
Of migrant traffic across the Mediterranean,

Mapping all the journeys from the Libyan coast,
Showing those boats that had made land in Syracuse,
But marking too the positions where boats had collapsed

Under the weight of their ill-fated cargo.
When you put on the headphones which dangled
From the tree's branches, a voice-over explained

How European governments had colluded in a
Plan to outlaw rescue boats so as to stem
The flow of migrants, a policy which effectively

Privatised rescue operations. The result,
Illustrated in a graph, was a dramatic
Rise in the numbers who drowned at sea.

There were too many examples to take in,
But in one typical case, when the SOS had been
Received by a trawler, rescue turned to catastrophe.

As the trawler approached the boat full of migrants
It turned unexpectedly, and in the resulting
Collision all but a handful of the passengers drowned.

The video finished with a blank black screen,
Taking its text from Dante, *Purgatorio XXXII*:
'O navicella mia, com' mal se' carca'

When I stood up, ready to move on, the
Others remained seated for some moments,
Perhaps still taking in the horror of what they'd seen.

I took the opportunity to slip off for a
Quiet smoke, where Marina wouldn't see me,
And found myself in a dark corner of the wood.

As I sat down to light my cigarette,
Taking the tar-rich smoke deep into my lungs,
I saw some car headlights up ahead in

A secluded avenue of poplars,
And as I looked more closely I made out
The shadowy form of a black limousine.

The car's silver hub-caps caught the light coming from
The lasers, and I saw they depicted monstrous heads
With a single horn protruding from their foreheads.

In the back seat there was a young African girl,
She can't have been more than fourteen years old,
Wearing the tight low-cut dress of a prostitute.

In the front seat, wearing a black suit and shades,
Sat a giant of a man, hidden behind a face mask, her minder,
Who glanced about nervously, and whenever

She opened her mouth, he'd lean over and slap her,
Telling her to shut the fuck up if she
Didn't want another taste of his fist.

When he saw me, loitering nearby, he must have
Realised I wasn't a potential client. He wound down
His window and spat contemptuously on the ground,

Then hit the gas, accelerating far off into the woods.

## CANTO XXXIII

When I'd made my way back to the crowd, I
Told the others what I'd seen. The dancers
Could scarcely believe what I was telling them:

'How is this possible, *here*, on the mount?'
One of them said, 'We should alert security at once!'
One of her companions burst into tears.

Yet as Marina stepped towards us, overhearing
What we were saying, she said we should not be
Surprised, that wherever migrants travelled

There were those who made it their business to
Exploit them, and they didn't care if they made
Their lives a misery so long as there was profit in it.

It was the same with the Giocherenda
In Palermo, she said, the Mafia were
Always round the corner waiting to abduct them.

And she explained that the reason there were
So few girls among the Giocherenda was that
Most of them were forced into the sex trade.

Then, in a whisper, she said: '*Modicum, et non*
*Videbitis me; et iterum,* my sisters,
*Modicum, et vos videbitis me.*'

Then she invited all three of them to step forward,
And told the rest of us to follow, myself,
The naturalist, and the remaining poet.

‘Where’s she taking us now?’ said Atkins, ‘I can’t
Make out a word she’s saying. Personally, I wouldn’t
Mind slipping off and catching some of the acts –

It’s been a long time since I heard any good music!’
‘I know what you mean,’ I said, ‘I could do with a
Bit more of The Fall, and The Pogues are on the bill.’

As she moved off, briskly, we followed dutifully, and
She had only gone a few paces before she
Caught my eye, and said: ‘Hurry along, so that

If I speak to you, you will be better placed
To hear what I say.’ And as I reached her side,
She added: ‘Well, don’t you have any questions for me?’

I’ve always been backwards in coming forward,
And so I was now, tongue-tied before her
Greater eloquence and intelligence.

‘You need to unwind a little,’ she said, ‘relax,
And stop wandering about as if you were in a dream.
You should be a bit more confident – it’s

Not every poet who gets to come up here.
Above all, you mustn’t let what you saw
Back there in the wood upset you too much.

As your talented son Louis put it, and if we
Hurry, we might just catch the end of his set,
“No one’s going to save the world, my friend,

But any one of us could make it better."
Putting it bluntly, nothing's perfect, but
Everyone on this mountain is doing their best

To make a change, whether it's those still stuck
On the slopes, or the artists whose work you've
Just seen up here, or those working in the seed bank.

Everyone has a simple choice – you can either
Look after number one, and let everything else go to Hell,
Or be part of the world in the widest sense.

And that means opening yourself up to
What you see around you, and showing respect.
You know Ovid – think of Erysichthon.

Whoever cuts down a forest or even snaps
Off the branch of a tree offends against the world.
In Ovid the offence is against Ceres

And the Dryads, but we now know that these things
Are just metaphors – though these metaphors
Make a lot more sense than neoliberal economics.

For cutting down the sacred grove of Ceres
Erysichthon suffered infinite insatiable
Hunger, awaking to grind his molars on air.

He emptied bowls heaped with food, but all he craved
For were bigger bowls heaped higher still, until he
Cashed in his own daughter, his last chattel, for food.

Take note: and as my words are carried from me,
Make sure that they are delivered to the living
Whose life is nothing but a race to death.

Now, don't think I didn't overhear what
You and your friend Atkins were saying just now.
We'll hear some music by and by, but first

I want to introduce you to some friends of mine.'
Leading the way, Marina took us past
A plantation of baobab trees and

Through a low leafy tunnel sculpted out of juniper,
Until we emerged behind a collection
Of tents. We stepped into one of these by

A concealed entrance in the back and at once
Emerged into a noisy crowd gathered there.
'This is the VIP tent,' she said, 'and

There are some people here you should meet,
Most of them are artists and activists, and
There should be a few people here from the LIP,

The London Institute of 'Pataphysics.
They were the people who put me on a
Committee to nominate a new raft of secular saints –

Look, here's Wilko Johnson, the great Blakeian,
Who we've nominated as the Saint of Canvey Island,
His name was put forward by Grevel Lindop.

And look – *Hello Marcia!* – here's the artist
Marcia Farquhar, a *Grande Gidouille* in the LIP.
She's going to be the mountain's next Artist-

In-Residence, after Grayson Perry, and here's
Her husband Jem Finer, an experimental
Composer and inventor, you've probably heard

About his *Longplayer*. Jem used to play
Banjo in The Pogues, and we persuaded him
To get the band back together for tonight.

Shane MacGowan should be here somewhere, if
He's not already plastered – we only just
Managed to get him out of Hell in time,

Under the Arts Council "Exceptional Talent" scheme…'
Marina was about to introduce us
To more people still – some puppet-makers

And clowns she'd met in Palestine, working
With refugees, when the crowd suddenly
Surged towards the music tent.

Something was happening, so we followed the wizards,
Then all of a sudden people were saying The Pogues
Were about to come on, so we didn't hang about.

I was glad we didn't, for as we stepped
Into the big top we heard the end of the set
By my son Lou Terry and Malachi Siner-Cheverst.

They were playing out with 'Cogs' on cello and guitar:
*'We're very small cogs in the scheme of things my friend,*
*But as important in that scheme as any other,*

*And no one's going to save the world my friend,*
*But any one of us could make it better.*
*Now look down at your feet and walk away from here,*

*Keep yourself but keep my words and follow your soul,*
*It never was easy to engineer*
*Different points of view swallow whole.*

*Stand there for a minute and let it take your breath away,*
*This moment I'm beside you,*
*I cannot stay…'*

Then it was The Pogues. We knew the Essex
Alp had magical powers, but to see
MacGowan up and running again at

Full throttle was a sight for sore eyes.
As they powered into their opening number
'The Sick Bed of Cuchulainn' the crowd went berserk.

MacGowan was headbutting his tambourine, as
In the good old days, spitting and cursing into the
Microphone, as if he was going to eat it for dinner.

Alp Angels were circulating with trays
Of space cakes – I took one and swallowed it,
After that everything was a blur.

I briefly remember Shane MacGowan
Crowd surfing, and Ronnie Blythe leaping out
Of the crowd ecstatically to join in,

And then I remember Tim and Marina
Taking to the stage together to sing
'Fairytale of New York' before some

Of the Alp Angels flew down from the wings
To eject some skinheads who were pushing their way in,
But after that it's all a blank.

We woke in morning dew, still drenched in sweat,
Like in the scene from *A Midsummer Night's Dream*.
The dancers were up first, and suggested we take a wash.

Then I noticed what I had not seen before:
In front of where they stood it was as if I saw
The Liffey and the Lagan rise together,

Then separate, like friends, unwillingly.
Then I noticed, too, that Marina once more
Stood at my side, already dressed and ready for the day,

And turning towards her, still half asleep,
I asked: 'What waters are these issuing from
One source, and then dividing self from self?'

She looked at me intensely, then said:
'Helen can explain, she's the expert.'
The naturalist looked puzzled at this,

Then whispered: 'I've explained it once to him already
Unless Lethe has totally erased his memory?'
And Marina: 'Perhaps those space cakes, as

Often happens, have dimmed his memory,
And taken the edge off his perceptions.
But don't worry, the waters of Eunoë

Will revive him and restore Mnemosyne's gift,
Go now, and take him to bathe in that,
Revive his weakened powers in its flow.'

Then, picking up a couple of towels,
The naturalist took me by the hand, and turning
To Atkins, said: 'Do you fancy coming along?'

Reader, if I had the space to write more, I'd tell
You, or try to tell you, just how refreshing
Those waters were – better than any jacuzzi.

But since all the pages designed for this
Second part of the poem have been filled,
The rules of art stop me in my tracks.

I got out of the water refreshed, as withered plants
Are renewed with new leaves. 'If we hurry,'
Said Helen, 'we can grab something to eat

With some of the artists you met last night in the
VIP tent. There's a great little vegan café
They all like.' So, I dried myself quickly, and

Flung on some clothes, ready to breakfast with the stars.

INDEX

## ACKNOWLEDGEMENTS

Thanks are due to the editors of *Translation and Literature*, *Golden Handcuffs Review* and *Junction Box* where parts of this poem were first published, in different form, and to Daragh O'Connell who gave me the opportunity to talk about the poem in progress at the Cork Centre for Dante Studies in Ireland. I would also like to thank all those who greeted *Dante's Inferno* with such warmth and encouraged me to keep going on what sometimes seemed like an impossible track. They include, in no particular order: Seamus Heaney, Tom Raworth, Marina Warner, John Ashbery, Tim Atkins, Jeff Hilson, Zoë Skoulding, Harry Mathews, Kimberly Campanello, Lily Robert-Foley, Oli Hazzard, Jèssica Pujol Duran, Steven Fowler, Colin Burrow, Matthew Reynolds, Adam Mars-Jones, Michael Schmidt, Cristina Fumagalli, George Ferzoco, Ralph Pite, Tristan Kay, Peter Hughes, Jeremy Noel-Tod, Alistair Elliot, Philip Davenport, Robert Sheppard, Anthony (Vahni) Capildeo, Ros Green, Adrian May, Geraldine Monk, Alan Halsey, Holly Pester, Jess Twyman, The Italian Cultural Institute, The London Review Bookshop, *The London Review of Books*, and many others whose names I forget as I write this.